W9-ATC-067

Attention-Deficit Hyperactivity Disorder

A Clinical Guide to Diagnosis and Treatment

Attention-Deficit Hyperactivity Disorder

A Clinical Guide to Diagnosis and Treatment

by

Larry B. Silver, M.D.

Clinical Professor of Psychiatry
and Director of Training in Child and Adolescent Psychiatry
at Georgetown University School of Medicine, Washington, D.C.

Washington, DC
London, England

Note: The author has worked to ensure that all information in this book concerning drug dosages, schedules, and routes of administration is accurate as of the time of publication and consistent with standards set by the U.S. Food and Drug Administration and the general medical community. As medical research and practice advance, however, therapeutic standards may change. For this reason and because human and mechanical errors sometimes occur, we recommend that readers follow the advice of a physician who is directly involved in their care or the care of a member of their family.

Books published by the American Psychiatric Press, Inc., represent the views and opinions of the individual authors and do not necessarily represent the policies and opinions of the Press or the American Psychiatric Association.

Copyright © 1992 American Psychiatric Press, Inc.
ALL RIGHTS RESERVED
Manufactured in the United States of America on acid-free paper.
95   6 5 4

American Psychiatric Press, Inc.
1400 K Street, N.W., Washington, DC 20005

Library of Congress Cataloging-in-Publication Data
Silver, Larry B.
    Attention-deficit hyperactivity disorder : a clinical guide to
diagnosis and treatment / by Larry B. Silver.
        p.   cm.
    Includes bibliographical references and index.
    ISBN 0-88048-509-4 (alk. paper)
    1. Attention deficit disorders—Diagnosis. 2. Hyperactive child
syndrome—Diagnosis. 3. Attention deficit disorders—Treatment.
4. Hyperactive child syndrome—Treatment.   I. Title.
    [DNLM: 1. Attention Deficit Disorder with Hyperactivity—
diagnosis. 2. Attention Deficit Disorder with Hyperactivity—
therapy.   WS 350.6 S587a]
RJ496.A86S55 1992
616.85′89—dc20
DNLM/DLC   91-4868
for Library of Congress   CIP

British Library Cataloguing in Publication Data
A CIP record is available from the British Library.

This book is dedicated to the memory of

Reginald S. Lourie, M.D.,

my teacher, mentor, and friend who taught me
the necessity of understanding
the total child in his or her total world.

Contents

Preface

School is the life work of children and adolescents. Thus anything that interferes with mastery and success in school will result in the student and family feeling stress. Attention-deficit hyperactivity disorder (ADHD) can be one of the reasons for academic and school difficulties.

In addition, ADHD can result in emotional or behavioral problems, difficulty with peer relationships, and difficulty within the family. Thus, unrecognized and untreated, this disorder will interfere greatly with all aspects of life.

Often, by the time a family brings its child to a health or mental health professional because of academic or school difficulties, there are multiple problems, and each must be identified and addressed. The emotional, social, and family problems may be the most apparent. Parents or teachers might report that the child or adolescent cannot sit still or is easily distracted and unable to stay on task. Lack of success in learning academic or study skills may also be found. These problems may be secondary to ADHD or may be secondary to the frequently associated disorder of learning disabilities.

Case example

John was 7 years old and in the first grade when his parents requested that I see him. He had significant behavioral problems at school as well as at home, and he had no friends.

The history provided by John's parents revealed that he had spent 2 years in preschool and an extra year in kindergarten because of "immaturity." The teachers' reports for these 4 years frequently referred to his inability to sit still and pay attention. It was these behaviors that were used to illustrate his immaturity. He was reported to have the same behaviors in first grade. The teacher described him as restless and often out of his seat. In addition, she said he never paid attention to her and never completed his work. His mother reported that when she did homework with him she had to remind him to pay attention. He was up and down. She commented, "The way I learn is not the way he learns."

John's parents gave a history of his chronic and pervasive hyperactivity, distractibility, and impulsivity. It was the impulsivity that caused problems at home. He constantly interrupted his mother, he fought with his sister, and he did "wild" things. For example, he would climb out on the roof or climb up on chairs to get things, or he would see something he wanted and dash for it, often bumping into things. Based on their observations, they noted that when he attempted to do his homework, he could not decode let alone understand what he read. He held his pencil in an awkward way to compensate for his lack of muscle control and still could not form all of his letters. He did not know his number facts nor could he count to 20.

During my sessions with John, he was fidgety and easily distracted by any sound, as well as by the pictures and other objects in my office. It was difficult for him to stay on task when talking or playing. His choice of play objects, play activities, and style of interacting were age appropriate. When I spoke of school, he became sad. John viewed himself as dumb and not as "good" (behaviorally) as the other children in his class. He had difficulty with easy, early first-grade reading, writing, and math tasks.

I called and spoke with his teacher again. She agreed that his skills were poor, especially for someone already a year older than the other first graders. She insisted that his difficulties were due to his immaturity saying, "If the parents made him act his age, he would do so much better."

I established the diagnosis of ADHD and started him on methylphenidate 5 mg tid; there was a dramatic improvement. His hyperactivity, distractibility, and impulsivity markedly decreased. The teacher reported a remarkable change in his behavior. She insisted that his change was due to my psychotherapy and had difficulty accepting the diagnosis but did admit that she had never heard of this disorder. John's parents also reported a major change; he was calm and pleasant at home. The sibling fighting stopped. He was able to sit and play by himself. He was able to do his homework. He played much better with the children in the neighborhood.

A full psychological and educational evaluation revealed major learning disabilities that clearly impacted on his academic ability. John's parents learned to be assertive with the school. They had him identified as learning disabled and had him receive the necessary services for this disability.

Parent counseling and brief therapy with John was initiated. As the parents better understood John's problems, they were able to modify their parenting behavior. As John better understood his problems and why he was taking medicine and getting special tutoring, he became happier and more pleasant. The behavioral problems at school and at home stopped. He related better to peers and developed several friendships.

If John's behaviors had been seen only as an oppositional defiant disorder and treated as such, progress would not have been made. Furthermore, such a diagnosis would have added support to the school staff's consistent misinterpretation of his behaviors. With the correct diagnoses and interventions, as well as the recognition that his emotional, social, and family problems were secondary to (not the cause of) the ADHD and the learning disabilities, progress was made and the problems significantly diminished.

The primary focus of this book is on ADHD. However, the related problems of learning disabilities and secondary emotional, social, and family problems must be understood and are therefore also discussed.

At present we are at a clinical "state of the art" rather than a "state of the science" when diagnosing and treating ADHD. In this book I incorporate the known literature but focus primarily on clinical experiences in working with such youth. To make the book more readable, I have chosen not to write it as a textbook with extensive references. Instead, it is a clinical guide with suggested readings for each chapter at the end of the book (Appendix A).

The treatment approaches are discussed from a clinical and practical perspective. This book is not meant as a substitute for the more detailed professional literature and information provided by the pharmaceutical manufacturers. Clinicians should use this book as a source of information and a clinical guide; however, each must incorporate her or his own clinical knowledge and judgment when working with children, adolescents, or adults.

It is hoped that this book will help you help the many people you see in your practice as well as their families.

Larry B. Silver, M.D.

INTRODUCTION

Chapter 1

Introduction

Attention-deficit hyperactivity disorder (ADHD) is the current term for a clinical problem physicians and other professionals have observed and handled for many years. Because the name and the understanding of this disorder have changed over the years, it is useful to start with a historical review.

History

In 1863 Heinrich Hoffman wrote a nursery rhyme about a boy who was restless, fidgety, hyperactive, and a behavioral problem to his family. Today, this boy might be identified as having ADHD.

"Phil, stop acting like a worm,
The table is no place to squirm."
thus speaks the father to his son,
severely says it, not in fun.
Mother frowns and looks around
although she doesn't make a sound.
But, Philipp will not take advise,
he'll have his way at any price.
He turns,
and churns,
he wiggles
and jiggles
Here and there on the chair;
"Phil, these twists I cannot bear."

Because ADHD is usually identified with school and academic difficulties, the history of this disorder in the United States starts with the study of children and adolescents with learning difficulties.

Before 1940, if children had difficulty learning, they were considered to be mentally retarded, emotionally disturbed, or socially or culturally disadvantaged. In the early 1940s, a fourth cause was identified: a nervous system disorder.

The initial researchers noted that these students had the same

3

learning problems as individuals known to have brain damage, yet they looked normal. It was therefore thought that these children also had brain damage but that the damage was minimal. The term minimal brain damage was introduced.

Another group of researchers felt that there was little evidence of brain damage. They believed that the problems related to "faulty wiring" within the brain: all of the brain mechanisms were present and operable; but some of the nerve pathways were not functioning correctly. This concept of faulty functioning, or dysfunction, became the accepted view, and the term minimal brain dysfunction (MBD) was coined.

In 1963, a committee was formed to review and present the current understanding of children with MBD. It was sponsored by the National Society for Crippled Children and Adults in cooperation with the Neurological and Sensory Diseases Service Program of the Division of Chronic Diseases of the U.S. Public Health Service. Later, the National Institute of Neurological Diseases and Blindness of the National Institutes of Health joined in this effort. The report on terminology and identification was published in 1966.

In this document, MBD was defined as "children of near-average, average, or above-average general intelligence with certain learning or behavioral disabilities ranging from mild to severe, which are associated with deviations of function of the central nervous system. These deviations may manifest themselves by various combinations of impairment in perception, conceptualization, language, memory, and control of attention, impulse, or motor function" (Clements S: Minimal Brain Dysfunction in Children: Terminology and Identification [National Institute of Neurological Diseases and Blindness Monograph No 3]. Washington, DC, U.S. Department of Health, Education and Welfare, 1966, p 9). Later in this document, the committee discussed emotional and social difficulties associated with this disorder. Thus using current concepts, this 1966 document defined MBD as children who had: 1) learning disabilities; 2) hyperactivity, distractibility, and impulsivity; and 3) emotional and social problems.

This overview of the problems was correct. However, it took another 20 years to understand them, during which time, researchers from a variety of professions studied children with MBD, each studying a different part of the problem and, thereby, introducing different terms. The result was confusion for professionals and parents.

Learning disabilities. Initially, researchers identified primary areas of difficulty in mastering basic academic skills and labeled the students accordingly. If the problems were with reading, the child had *dyslexia*; with writing, *dysgraphia*; and with arithmetic, *dyscalculia*. Later, an effort was made to understand what caused these specific learning difficulties. Today we refer to the child or adolescent with a presumed neurological basis for his or her learning difficulties as having a learning disability.

Hyperactivity and distractibility. Descriptions of the overactive child date back to the Old Testament. In the United States, the concept was cited in literature for the first time in 1937 when Bradley, a pediatrician, described children who were recovering from viral encephalitis as hyperactive or distractible. The first official acceptance of what is now called ADHD as a clinical diagnostic category was in 1968 with the publication of the Second Edition of the Diagnostic and Statistical Manual of Mental Disorders (DSM-II). The term "hyperkinetic reaction of childhood (or adolescence)" was used, and with it came the concept of the "hyperactive child." The disorder was characterized by "overactivity, restlessness, distractibility, and a short attention span, especially in young children; the behavior usually diminished in adolescence" (American Psychiatric Association: Diagnostic and Statistical Manual of Mental Disorders, 2nd Edition. Washington, DC, American Psychiatric Association, 1968, p 50).

In DSM-III the term for this disorder was changed to attention deficit disorder (ADD) to emphasize that distractibility and a short attention span were the primary clinical issues and that hyperactivity or impulsivity also might be present. Two subtypes of this disorder were defined: ADD with hyperactivity and ADD without hyperactivity. The definition for ADD with hyperactivity noted that "the child displays, for his or her mental and chronological age, signs of developmentally inappropriate inattention, impulsivity, and hyperactivity" (American Psychiatric Association: Diagnostic and Statistical Manual of Mental Disorders, 3rd Edition. Washington, DC, American Psychiatric Association, 1980, p 43).

For a patient to be diagnosed with this disorder, the onset of the behaviors had to have occurred before age 7, and the behaviors had to have been present for at least 6 months. DSM-III listed behaviors characteristic of each component—inattention, impulsivity, and hyperactivity. To establish the diagnosis, the child had to show evidence of at least one of these three behaviors.

In DSM-III-R, the revised edition of DSM-III, the term was changed to attention-deficit hyperactivity disorder to reflect that, although distractibility is the primary issue, hyperactivity is also an important factor of the disorder. The diagnosis still requires that the onset occur before age 7, but now the child or adolescent has to exhibit at least 8 of a list of 14 behaviors for at least 6 months. These behaviors are discussed in Chapter 3.

The committee preparing DSM-IV, scheduled to be published in 1992, is currently considering several issues:

- Should ADHD be listed under the general category of disruptive behavior disorders?
- Because research data suggest that children with distractibility only have a different outcome than those who have hyperactivity or impulsivity, should there be two different terms, perhaps in two different categories?
- Should attention-deficit disorder without hyperactivity be listed under the specific developmental disorders and attention-deficit hyperactivity disorder be listed under the disruptive behavioral disorders?

It is hoped that as research in neurology adds new understanding to the concept of ADHD specifically, and to the broader concept of attentional disorders, this diagnostic category will be further clarified.

Emotional, social, and family problems. For children and adolescents with ADHD plus possibly a learning disability, school becomes frustrating. They may display emotional or behavioral problems in school. Moreover, they often develop peer and other social problems. Hence family members become frustrated, and parents may disagree on the best approach to raising and disciplining their child. Unfortunately, over time, the superficial problems are the only ones seen; behavioral and academic problems at school are considered to be a result of the emotional and family problems. In reality, however, these problems are not the *cause* but the *consequence* of the difficulties at school, which result in frustration and failure. It is this differentiation between cause and consequence that must be stressed with children and adolescents who have ADHD.

Prevalence of ADHD

Because of the changing criteria for establishing the diagnosis of ADHD and the absence of a reliable or valid diagnostic method, no clear data are available. When similar rating scales are used and teachers are used as the raters, the prevalence of ADHD in the school-aged population appears to range from 10 to 20%. If parents are the source of the information, the prevalence rates are higher, perhaps as high as 30%.

Studies have shown that ADHD is more common among boys, with the boy to girl ratio reported to be from 2:1 to 10:1 in clinic-referred samples. However, the proportion among nonreferred children appears to be closer to 3:1. This higher rate of males among clinic samples as compared with community surveys probably reflects referral bias. Males are more likely than females to be aggressive and antisocial, and such behavior is more likely to lead to a referral. It also may be that these data reflect the underidentification of ADHD in girls.

Despite attentional problems similar to those of boys with ADHD, girls with ADHD tend to be less intrusive and exhibit fewer aggressive symptoms. Thus these symptoms in girls are less likely to come to the teacher's (or other professional's) attention. It is possible, therefore, that the group of students most often not recognized, referred, or diagnosed are girls with distractibility.

Life History of ADHD

The longitudinal data are even less complete for all of the reasons discussed above. In addition, the concept of ADHD in adults is relatively new and thus not followed until recently.

Current data suggest that about 50% of children with ADHD show a decrease or loss of the behaviors at puberty. The reason for this improvement is not known. Fifty percent will continue to have ADHD into adolescence, and between 30 and 70% of children with ADHD will continue to have these behaviors into adulthood.

The Total Child

We have now returned to the descriptions and perspectives noted in the 1966 monograph on MBD. Only we now understand that such children and adolescents have a group of problems that are often found together. Nearly all of them have a learning disability, some of them have ADHD, and most of them develop *secondary* emotional, social, and family problems.

We do know more about the frequency with which these problems occur. It has been estimated that of all children and adolescents with learning disabilities, 20–25% also have ADHD. On the other hand, for children who have ADHD, there is a 50–80% chance that they also have a learning disability. Thus when a physician establishes a diagnosis of ADHD, it is critical that he or she explore the possibility of the patient also having a learning disability. From a preventive medicine view, *the clinician must rule out a learning disability with each patient diagnosed as having ADHD.*

Children and adolescents with ADHD often develop emotional, social, and family problems. If they also have a learning disability, the probability of developing such problems increases.

Summary

ADHD and learning disabilities are related disorders, but they are not the same disorder. A learning disability impacts on the basic psychological processes needed to learn. ADHD results in behaviors that can make the individual unavailable for the learning experience. The medications that treat ADHD will not correct the learning disability. The special education approaches used to treat the learning disabilities will not improve the ADHD. Some professionals and parents still use these terms interchangeably. This should not be done.

ADHD is a *life disability*. Hyperactivity, distractibility, and impulsivity are not just school problems; they are life problems. These behaviors interfere with classroom learning and behavior. They also interfere with family life, peer interactions, and all other activities. This concept is important to consider when deciding on a treatment approach. For example, if the clinician treats the ADHD during school hours and months only, the individual might do well in school but continue to have a behavioral problem at home and with friends.

ADHD can also be a *life-time disability*. About 50% of children with ADHD will continue to have this disorder into adolescence. (Only about half appear to improve with the brain maturational spurt at puberty.) Of adolescents with ADHD, it is estimated that between 30 and 70% will continue to have ADHD as an adult. Adult (or residual) ADHD is an established concept. We once believed (or wished) that these children outgrew their problems at puberty; we now know that this is not true for all.

ADHD is a complex clinical problem. It is critical for the clinician to be aware of the total child or adolescent in his or her total world when planning treatment. It is equally critical that any related disorder—learning disabilities or secondary emotional, social, and family problems—be recognized and treated as well.

DIAGNOSIS

Chapter 2

Presenting Clinical Problems Suggesting Attention-Deficit Hyperactivity Disorder

The essential features of attention-deficit hyperactivity disorder (ADHD) as noted in DSM-III-R are "developmentally inappropriate degrees of inattention, impulsiveness, and hyperactivity. People with the disorder generally display some disturbances in each of these areas, but to varying degrees" (American Psychiatric Association: Diagnostic and Statistical Manual of Mental Disorders, 3rd Edition, Revised. Washington, DC, American Psychiatric Association, 1987, p 50). However, some will have one and some two of these behaviors. *It is not necessary to have all three behaviors.* Children can be relaxed, even hypoactive, and have ADHD if they are distractible and/or impulsive.

What Are These Behaviors?

Hyperactivity. In the past, we described hyperactive children as those who ran around and could not stand or sit still. "If you went out to your waiting room and it was in shambles, you knew you had a hyperactive child." We now know that most children with ADHD are not that obviously active. They are more likely to be fidgety; some part of their body is always in motion, often a purposeless motion. Their fingers are tapping, or they are playing with their pencil. While sitting, their legs are swinging or they are twisting or squirming in their chair. Teachers may report that they sit with one knee on the floor. Parents may report that their child has never sat still through a whole meal. Some appear to be verbally hyperactive, talking constantly.

Distractibility. Children with ADHD have difficulty knowing what to attend to in their environment versus what to block out. All stimuli come and may be focused on. Therefore, these children are distractible; they have difficulty sustaining attention (thus a short attention span) and difficulty completing a task.

Children with ADHD may be auditorily and/or visually distractible. If the individual is auditorily distractible, he or she will hear and respond to sounds that most others would hear and tune out. Teachers report that if someone in the back of the room is tapping a pencil or talking, others can ignore it but the auditorily distractible child must turn and listen. If someone is talking in the hall or someone is dribbling a basketball outside on the playground, this student looks up and asks, "What's that?" Parents report that when they are reading a story to their children or they are doing homework, every sound (a floorboard creaking in another room or a car horn a block away) elicits a response.

Visually distractible children may by distracted by the design on a rug or a picture or other objects in the room. If outside, they will notice birds flying, clouds going by, or the trees and not stay focused on the appropriate activity. Parents might report that when sent to get something, their child sees something along the way and starts to play with it. Then something else is seen, the child goes to it, and the original task is never completed.

Some children who are distractible appear to be able to attend to certain tasks for long periods of time. Parents may question if their child is distractible if he or she can spend hours watching television or playing a video game. These tasks are usually ones that are enjoyable and where the motivation is high. It appears that to be able to focus like this, these individuals have to apply extra "filters" to block out superfluous stimuli. They appear to be in a trance. Parents report they can talk to these children, but they do not respond. To get their attention, the parents must shake them or stand between them and the activity. Then, they may say "huh?" and respond.

Some adolescents with distractibility insist that they can study best with music playing in the background. Parents question how these individuals could be distractible if they can work with such noise. However, so many adolescents have used the same explanation, that I now believe they may be right. They say that if the room is very quiet, they hear every little sound. Background music, however, blocks out these sounds; all they hear is the steady sound of the music. They believe that they are less distracted and are better able to work.

Parents may also report that their child experiences what I term "sensory overload." The noise and bustle of birthday parties, shopping malls, circuses, and sports events can cause these children to become upset and irritable. They might cover their ears or want to leave, or they might complain of a headache. It appears that if there is too much auditory stimulation, they cannot block out the input and they feel overloaded. Adolescents and young adults may describe the same experience at a party or in a bar. The music playing and people talking cause an auditory overload, and they feel uncomfortable or anxious.

Impulsivity. Individuals with impulsivity appear to not be able to reflect before they speak or act. Thus they do not learn from experience because they cannot delay their action long enough to recall past experiences and consequences. They start to say something and may be sorry they said it before they are finished. When they get upset, they react spontaneously by hitting or throwing something, or they turn quickly and knock things over. They may fail to wait for their turn and speak out or may answer a question before the teacher completes it. Because of this impulsive behavior, they appear to have poor judgment and may be accident prone. Parents even have been accused of child abuse because of frequent injuries to their child due to these impulsive behaviors.

There are several clinical problems that may be seen with children and adolescents who are impulsive, including bed-wetting, firesetting and fascination with or playing with fire, and stealing. Lying more than is age-appropriate or hiding or hoarding food in their room may also be seen. There is no clear explanation for the association of these behaviors with impulsivity. However, when obtaining the patient's history, questions should be asked to determine if these behaviors are present.

How Is Information on Behavior Obtained?

It is difficult for physicians to observe hyperactivity, distractibility, or impulsivity during a professional office visit. Patients are usually seen for only 5–7 minutes. Children with ADHD may have learned to be quiet and attentive in the office setting to avoid being stuck, gagged, or poked. If the office is that of a mental health professional, the room is likely to be quiet with a one-to-one interaction with an adult. Thus if ADHD behaviors are not seen in the office, the professional should not conclude that they do not exist.

The best source of observational data is from in vivo situations. The parents, teachers, tutors, and other adults who interact with these individuals can describe their behaviors in structured and unstructured settings: at school, in the home, and with friends. If realistic, a visit to the school to observe is helpful. If this is not possible, the clinician should talk to the teachers or ask the parents to get observational information from them. There are rating scales and other informational forms that parents and teachers can use to quantify the observations. Such data can help in the diagnostic process. These instruments will be discussed in Chapter 3.

All That Looks Like ADHD Is Not ADHD

There are many reasons why children and adolescents can be hyperactive, distractible, and/or impulsive. However, not all individuals who display these behaviors have ADHD. Related disorders also can cause these behaviors. This concept will be introduced here and detailed in Chapter 3.

Learning disabilities. As mentioned earlier, there is a high probability that individuals with ADHD will also have learning disabilities. The behaviors caused by the learning disabilities can look like ADHD. For example, in DSM-III-R, the following descriptions of ADHD could be a reflection of a learning disability: not finishing class work, having difficulty organizing work, appearing not to be listening, and doing sloppy work. In Chapter 3, this differential diagnostic process is expanded to include specific types of learning disabilities that could clinically present like ADHD.

Emotional problems. Anxiety or depression can be expressed by behaviors of increased motor activity, inattentiveness or distractibility, or irritability and impulsivity. In addition, children and adolescents with an oppositional defiant disorder or conduct disorder may appear to have ADHD or may indeed have ADHD as well. It is important, therefore, to decide if the observed behaviors are a result of primary emotional or behavioral problems, emotional or behavioral problems secondary to ADHD plus possible learning disabilities, or ADHD. The differential diagnostic process needed to clarify these issues is discussed in Chapter 3.

Summary

It is possible that too many children and adolescents are diagnosed as having ADHD. This may be because clinicians diagnose all individuals presenting with hyperactivity, distractibility, and impulsivity as having ADHD without exploring other possible causes. Likewise it is possible that too many children and adolescents who are hyperactive, distractible, and/or impulsive are not diagnosed properly as having ADHD because clinicians see the presenting emotional, social, and family problems and establish a psychiatric diagnosis without considering whether these problems are secondary to ADHD plus a possible learning disability. Chapter 3 focuses on the importance of differential diagnosis for patients with these behaviors.

Chapter 3

Establishing the Diagnosis

Presently there are no formal tests to establish the diagnosis of attention-deficit hyperactivity disorder (ADHD). There are no specific physical or neurological findings that establish the diagnosis. There are excellent rating scales that can identify if an individual is hyperactive, distractible, and/or impulsive; however, these rating scales may not differentiate between ADHD and other possible causes for these behaviors. Therefore, the best diagnostic technique is the clinical history, which must include observational data from the school and family.

As discussed in Chapters 1 and 2, there are many possible causes of hyperactivity, distractibility, and/or impulsivity in children and adolescents. Moreover, many individuals with ADHD also have a learning disability, and certain types of learning disabilities can result in hyperactive or distractible behaviors. The differential diagnostic process must include a consideration of all possible causes of the observed hyperactive, distractible, and/or impulsive behaviors.

Perhaps the reason too many children and adolescents are diagnosed as having ADHD is because this differential diagnostic thinking is not done. A teacher tells a parent that a child cannot sit still or stay on task, the parent goes to a physician, and the physician prescribes medication. The assumption is that all children who are hyperactive or distractible have ADHD. In this chapter, other possible causes of these behaviors are reviewed and the approach to establishing the diagnosis is discussed.

DSM-III-R Criteria for ADHD

The diagnosis of ADHD is to be considered if the three criteria in Table 3–1 are met. However, I believe that there are problems with the DSM-III-R criteria. First, each of the behaviors listed could be caused by an emotional problem, a learning disability, or environmental influences. Second, recent research suggests that ADHD may be only one aspect of a group of attentional disorders. Thus a broader clinical concept may be needed. For now, however, DSM-III-R is the official diagnostic manual, and its criteria should be used.

Table 3–1. **Diagnostic criteria of attention-deficit hyperactivity disorder**

A. A disturbance of at least 6 months during which at least eight of the following are present:

  1) often fidgets with hands or feet or squirms in seat (in adolescents, may be limited to subjective feelings of restlessness)
  2) has difficulty remaining seated when required to do so
  3) is distracted easily by extraneous stimuli
  4) has difficulty awaiting turn in games or group situations
  5) often blurts out answers to questions before they have been completed
  6) has difficulty following through on instructions from others (not due to oppositional behavior or failure of comprehension), e.g., fails to finish chores
  7) has difficulty sustaining attention in tasks or play activities
  8) often shifts from one uncompleted activity to another
  9) has difficulty playing quietly
  10) often talks excessively
  11) often interrupts or intrudes on others, e.g., butts into other children's games
  12) often does not seem to listen to what is being said to him or her
  13) often loses things necessary for tasks or activities at school or at home (e.g., toys, pencils, books, assignments)
  14) often engages in physically dangerous activities without considering possible consequences (not for the purpose of thrill-seeking), e.g., runs into street without looking

B. Onset before the age of seven years.

C. Does not meet the criteria for a pervasive developmental disorder.

Source. American Psychiatric Association: Diagnostic and Statistical Manual of Mental Disorders, 3rd Edition, Revised. Washington, DC, American Psychiatric Association, 1987, pp 52–53. Used with permission.

The Differential Diagnostic Process

The three presenting behaviors—hyperactivity, distractibility, and impulsivity—are reviewed here. A discussion of their possible causes follows.

Hyperactivity. Most hyperactive children and adolescents are not running around the room or jumping on the furniture. Instead, they appear to be fidgety, tapping their fingers, moving their pencils, swinging their legs, and getting up and down from their desk or the dinner table. Something is always in motion. Parents may report that the child is equally restless at night, moving about the bed. With adolescents, the fidgety behaviors may be less apparent, but they are there.

Distractibility. It is important to look at the many reasons for distractibility. I feel these reasons fall into one of two general groups: internal distractibility and external distractibility. Reasons for internal distractibility include daydreaming, auditory perception disability, and cognitive disinhibition. Those for external distractibility include environmental overload and ADHD.

Daydreaming is not uncommon among children and adolescents. As students, they sometimes escape into their thoughts and then realize that they have not heard a word the teacher was saying. The teacher might comment that such students are not paying attention, but daydreaming may reflect family or other stress, an emotional disorder, or simply the excitement of an event (such as on the day before a holiday or vacation).

Auditory perception disabilities are discussed in detail in Chapter 4. Children with such a disability may have difficulty with what is called an auditory figure-ground problem. That is, if there is more than one sound in the environment (students talking, activity in the hall, or a teacher talking), they may have difficulty knowing which sounds to listen to. Teachers might be into their third sentence before these students realize they are talking. By then the students are lost and are subsequently described as not paying attention.

Another auditory perception disability is called an "auditory lag." Individuals with this disability need to concentrate on what they hear for an instant longer than others do before it is understood (perceived). Thus they must concentrate simultaneously on what they just heard while trying to hold on to what is coming in next. They cannot keep up this process and eventually miss parts of what is said. For example, the teacher reviews a lesson plan. As soon as the teacher has finished, these students ask questions on the information just discussed and are then accused of not paying attention.

Some individuals have difficulty inhibiting their internal thought processes. (There is no established term for this difficulty; I call it cognitive disinhibition.) Their internal thoughts protrude into their conscious behaviors. For example, in class they suddenly start talking about something that appears to be off the topic—younger children might suddenly start talking about dinosaurs or space—or they might begin to laugh or become upset by their internal thoughts. This disorder is most often found among individuals with pervasive developmental disorder. However, before this disorder is identified, these children may be described as easily distractible and unable to stay on task.

The best example of an environmental overload occurred when many educational systems decided that the "open classroom" would create a more stimulating environment for learning. For many normal students the noise and multiple auditory inputs created distractibility. They could not pay attention to their teacher or their work. The stimulation of the many work stations, both in their classroom and in adjacent spaces, often became visually overstimulating and caused distractibility. These students did not have ADHD, but they appeared to be distractible.

For some students, sitting next to a window that is open or to a door that is open to the hall can be distracting. For other students, a classroom that the teacher cannot control—one that is noisy or has students moving around—can be too much of a sensory overload to permit attending to a task. The same situation might exist for students who like to do their homework in the family room with the television playing and siblings running around or talking.

Impulsivity. Impulsivity is described as the inability (or difficulty with being able) to stop and reflect before speaking or acting. Impulsive individuals interrupt teachers and parents, answer questions with the first thought that occurs, or say things that they immediately regret saying. They may get frustrated or angry and yell, throw things, or hit people. Furthermore, they never learn from experience because to learn from experience one must stop and think about past experiences and consequences before speaking or acting. The impulsive individual does not have the luxury of time to think first.

Impulsivity is characteristic of many psychiatric disorders and can reflect immaturity, anxiety, depression, or learned (and possibly rewarded) behavior. This behavior might also reflect an immature or dysfunctional nervous system. One such dysfunction is ADHD.

Differential Diagnosis

Emotional Issues

Anxiety. The most common cause of hyperactivity, distractibility, or impulsivity in children, adolescents, and adults is anxiety. Anxiety can be a reflection of psychological stress or conflict or of a specific psychiatric disorder. If these three behaviors are a reflection of anxiety, the diagnosis is *not* ADHD. When people are anxious, they can be restless and motorically active. For children, motor activity might be the primary way of expressing anxiety. In addition, it is difficult for people to pay attention when they feel anxious. They may day-dream or attempt to watch television or read a book. However, it is difficult to stay on the task or to pay attention to what is heard, seen, or read. Anxiety can cause an individual to be irritable and therefore appear impulsive.

Depression. The next most common cause of hyperactivity, distractibility, or impulsivity with children, adolescents, or adults is depression. Depression might reflect a psychological conflict or stress or might reflect a specific psychiatric disorder. If these behaviors are a reflection of a depressive process, the diagnosis is *not* ADHD. Depression can occur at any age and may be manifested in an agitated or withdrawn form (psychomotor retardation). Individuals who are agitated may be restless and active and may experience difficulty concentrating or staying on task. Some may be irritable and act impulsively. In the withdrawn phase of depression, individuals may be so involved with their feelings and thoughts that it is difficult for them to pay attention to what is going on or to communicate with others.

Case example

Chris was 10 years old and in the fifth grade when brought in for a consultation. He had been in individual and group therapy for 2 years because of his emotional problems. He was unhappy in school and not doing his school work in class or at home. A psychological and education evaluation done by his school system 18 months earlier showed evidence of visual perception, visual motor, and fine motor difficulties. However, the evaluation team concluded, "his weaknesses were not great enough nor his skill levels behind enough to qualify for services."

A review of his school records plus the history provided by his parents revealed that Chris had been labeled as hyperactive and distractible in preschool and kindergarten. His first-grade teacher described him as overactive and unable to stay on task. His second-grade teacher made the same comments. Third grade was described as a terrible year; he got into fights, disrupted the classroom, and did not complete his work. Fourth grade was similar. He was falling further behind in school skills and strategies. The teachers blamed this on his *refusal* to sit still and pay attention.

The history added to the diagnostic process. Chris was adopted by his family at age 4. He had been placed in a foster home for 1 year before this adoption because his mother's boyfriend had sexually abused him. She was also neglectful, often leaving him home alone. The social agency history indicated that she had used alcohol and drugs during this pregnancy. Chris had been placed in individual and group therapy to help him cope with his past. All of his academic and behavioral problems were viewed by his therapists as secondary to his emotional problems.

During my psychiatric assessment sessions with Chris, he spoke openly of his past. He knew about it and felt that it no longer bothered him. "I talked it all over in my therapy. It is behind me and this is my family now and forever. I like them." I could find no evidence of emotional conflicts related to his past. He did speak of his frustrations in school; he did not like school, and he knew he was not as smart as the other kids. Chris was aware that it was difficult to sit still in class, and he knew that he was easily distracted by any noise or activity. He blamed the fighting on the other kids teasing him.

Chris showed a chronic and pervasive history (as far as such a history could be obtained) of hyperactivity and distractibility. Thus the diagnosis *could* be ADHD. The pregnancy history of alcohol and substance abuse might support an organic problem manifested by ADHD and learning disabilities. However, other factors in his history suggested that he was still dealing with what might be called a posttraumatic stress disorder secondary to his early childhood history. The hyperactivity and distractibility might be a reflection of his anxiety or depression.

After discussing the issues with his therapist, I presented the diagnostic questions to Chris and his parents in a family session. We agreed to a trial of medication to help clarify the issues. He was started on methylphenidate, 5 mg tid.

From the first dose, he was calmer, less distractible, and better able to stay on task. His teachers and his parents noticed a significant improvement. After I made several contacts with his school system, Chris was identified as learning disabled and placed in a special education program. With this change in program and the use of the medication, the fighting and other behavioral problems at school stopped.

Behavioral Issues

It is estimated that about 50% of children who meet the DSM-III-R criteria for ADHD will meet the DSM-III-R criteria for an oppositional defiant disorder or a conduct disorder. Similarly, most children who meet the criteria for these disruptive behavioral disorders will meet the criteria for ADHD. The critical question is whether these are separate disorders that coexist in the same child (comorbidity) or whether they represent different phenotypic manifestations of the same underlying disorder.

The issue is confused further by referral bias. If the definition of ADHD is established on the basis of the symptomatology of children referred to mental health centers, then it is likely that an oppositional defiant or conduct disorder will be prominent. This will have the effect of a self-fulfilling prophecy by further encouraging educators to identify ADHD on the basis of these disruptive behavioral problems.

Recent research supports the belief that ADHD should be differentiated from oppositional defiant or conduct disorders. Evidence shows that children can have these disorders independently, but that they are more likely to occur in combination with each other. Each disorder must be identified and addressed in the treatment plan.

Oppositional defiant disorder. The DSM-III-R diagnostic criteria for an oppositional defiant disorder are listed in Table 3–2. The essential feature of this disorder is a recurring pattern of negativistic, hostile, and defiant behavior that has become developmentally stable for at least 6 months. These symptoms must be present to a degree that is excessive or deviant for the child's mental age.

Some believe that there is a link between early oppositional defiant disorder and later conduct disorder. During the preschool years, the oppositional behavior is most often seen in the home environment. It may not be noted in the school environment until middle childhood. The pattern of hostile and defiant behavior is most evident in interactions with adults and peers that the child knows well and may not appear at all with strangers or with clinicians during office evaluations. Over time, this disorder evolves from oppositional behavior toward parents to hostile and aggressive behavior toward others,

---

Table 3–2. Diagnostic criteria for oppositional defiant disorder

A. A disturbance of at least 6 months during which at least five of the following symptoms are present:
1) often loses temper
2) often argues with adults
3) often actively defies or refuses adult requests or rules (e.g., refuses to do chores at home)
4) often deliberately does things that annoy other people (e.g., grabs other children's hats)
5) often blames others for his or her own mistakes
6) often touchy or annoyed easily by others
7) often angry and resentful
8) often spiteful or vindictive
9) often swears or uses obscene language

B. Does not meet the criteria for conduct disorder, and does not occur exclusively during the course of a psychotic disorder, dysthymia, or a major depressive, hypomanic, or manic episode.

Source. American Psychiatric Association: Diagnostic and Statistical Manual of Mental Disorders, 3rd Edition, Revised. Washington, DC, American Psychiatric Association, 1987, pp 57–58. Used with permission.

to antisocial acts within the community, and finally, possibly, into covert, clandestine criminal behavior as seen in a conduct disorder.

Conduct disorder. It is not uncommon for a child to be diagnosed ADHD in early childhood, then as oppositional defiant disorder in later childhood, and finally as conduct disorder in late childhood or early adolescence.

The DSM-III-R criteria for conduct disorder (Table 3–3) indicate that the essential feature of this disorder is a persistent pattern of conduct in which the basic rights of others and major age-appropriate societal norms or rules are violated. It is usually pervasive, occurring in school, the community, with peers, and at home. Physical aggression and physical destructiveness are more common among persons with this disorder than those with an oppositional defiant disorder.

Three types of conduct disorder are identified in DSM-III-R: group type (occurring as a group activity with peers), solitary aggressive type (physically aggressive behavior occurring in isolation from a peer

Table 3–3. **Diagnostic criteria for conduct disorder**

A. A disturbance of conduct lasting at least 6 months, during which at least three of the following symptoms have been present:
 1) has stolen without confrontation of a victim on more than one occasion (including forgery)
 2) has run away from home overnight at least twice while living in parental or parental surrogate home (or once without returning)
 3) often lies (other than to avoid physical or sexual abuse)
 4) has deliberately engaged in fire-setting
 5) is often truant from school (for older person, absent from work)
 6) has broken into someone else's house, building, or car
 7) has deliberately destroyed others' property (other than by fire-setting)
 8) has been physically cruel to animals
 9) has forced someone into sexual activity with him or her
10) has used a weapon in more than one fight
11) often initiates physical fights
12) has stolen with confrontation of a victim (e.g., mugging, purse-snatching, extortion, armed robbery)
13) has been physically cruel to people
B. If 18 or older, does not meet criteria for Antisocial Personality Disorder.

Source.   American Psychiatric Association: Diagnostic and Statistical Manual of Mental Disorders, 3rd Edition, Revised. Washington, DC, American Psychiatric Association, 1987, p 55. Used with permission.

group), and undifferentiated type (does not overlap with either of the other types).

Neurological Factors Other Than ADHD

Learning Disability

One type of a learning disability, an auditory perception disability, was discussed earlier in this chapter. Children and adolescents with such a disability can present as distractible. Other types of learning disabilities might make it difficult for them to understand, organize their work, or complete school assignments. Such students may appear not to be staying on task when the real issue is that they are on task but cannot do the work. If students with a learning disability do not understand the work and cannot do the work, they may become anxious, and this anxiety can cause hyperactive or distractible behavior. In this case, it is the anxiety caused by the learning disability, not ADHD, that is causing the behaviors.

Sometimes the diagnosis of ADHD is made correctly, these students are started on the appropriate medication, and the hyperactivity and/or distractibility decrease. However, the associated learning disability may not have been diagnosed. Suddenly, these students can sit in class and attend to their work, but they do not understand the work and cannot do it. They become anxious and start to fidget or daydream. The teacher might believe that the medication is no longer working. Hence it is important to understand that even if on the proper medication, children and adolescents can become anxious or depressed.

Sensory Integrative Disorder

Some individuals with a learning disability also have a sensory integrative disorder. This disorder will be discussed in more detail in Chapter 4. Briefly, these individuals have difficulty receiving and processing perceptions that are needed to orient and use their body in space. The three perceptions affected by this disorder are the tactile, proprioception, and vestibular systems. These individuals may be tactically sensitive or defensive, they may have difficulty moving their body appropriately in space or in performing tasks that require motor planning (e.g., buttoning or tying), or they may have difficulty orienting their body to their head position. If tactically sensitive or defensive, they may be overly aware of tags on their cloths, a belt, or the texture of their cloths; thus they may wiggle or move about, appearing to be hyperactive. They might be unsure of their body and its position in space; thus they might move about, trying to become more comfortable. Children with a sensory integrative disorder thus might be fidgety. In these situations, the hyperactivity and fidgety behaviors are a reflection of this disorder and not of ADHD.

Rating Scales as Part of the Diagnostic Process

Rating scales are popular when assessing children's behaviors. In addition to the clinical interview, these behavioral rating scales provide information from people who know the child well (such as parents and teachers); they are efficient and are based on normative dataz.

The question is, what is being measured or assessed? As noted earlier, the data from a rating scale might show the individual to be hyperactive, distractible, and/or impulsive, but the clinician may still not know why these behaviors are present. Thus if rating scales are used, they must be considered a source of observational data to be used as part of the diagnostic process, but not the diagnostic process itself.

There are advantages to using rating scales in clinical practice. First, there are normative data that permit the clinician to determine the degree of deviance displayed by a particular child within the population of same-age and same-sex children. This is essential to the diagnosis of ADHD since many ADHD characteristics occur to some degree in normal children. Second, rating scales can be a convenient means for collapsing information about a child across situations and time intervals into units of information of value to diagnosis. It would be difficult to collect, for clinical purposes, direct observations of a child over diverse settings during a span of several months. Finally, rating scales provide a convenient means for evaluating a person's responses to clinical interventions.

Parent-Rating Scales

The Conners series of parent-rating scales have been the most widely used. There are three forms: the original 93-item version, the revised 48-item version, and the 10-item Abbreviated Symptom Questionnaire. However, because these scales were developed during the time that DSM-II was in use, the focus is primarily on hyperactivity.

The Child Behavioral Checklist by Achenbach and Edelbrock was developed in 1983 and is also widely used. It has a hyperactivity factor, but there is no factor related to distractibility.

New instruments have been developed that address the DSM-III-R criteria, including the Child Attention Problems by Barkley, the ADHD

Rating Scale by DuPaul, and the Attention Deficit Disorders Evaluation Scale by McCarney.

Teacher-Rating Scales

The Conners teacher-rating scales are most widely used. There are several versions. Again, the primary focus is on hyperactivity. The Conners Abbreviated Syndrome Questionnaire, developed by Conners and Barkley, is a 10-item list; however, it assesses general misconduct and aggression rather than inattention and other specific ADHD symptoms.

The Child Attention Problems (CAP) rating scale, developed by Edelbrock from the Teacher Report Form of the Child Behavior Checklist (by Achenbach and Edelbrock), contains 12 items that specifically assess inattention and overactivity.

Newer Rating Instruments

The Yale Children's Inventory is a parent-based rating scale that assesses multiple factors related to ADHD and associated disorders. Its 11 scales measure attention; impulsivity; activity; tractability; habituation; conduct disorder, socialized; conduct disorder, aggressive; negative affect; language; fine motor; and academics. Thus an effort is made to identify hyperactivity, distractibility, and impulsivity, as well as to search for evidence of an emotional disorder or a learning difficulty.

Diagnosis

The clinical history and observational data are the best methods available to help the clinician to establish the diagnosis of ADHD. The history is obtained from the parents, the current teachers, the school records, and other significant adults (e.g., scout leaders and religious educators). The observations should include the school and the home environment.

If the history of the behaviors of hyperactivity, distractibility, and/or impulsivity relate to specific times in the individual's life or to specific spaces or activities, anxiety should be considered as the possible cause (e.g., "Billy was never described as hyperactive until third grade" "Joan is only distractible in math class" or "Bob is only impulsive after his father gets home at night"). These behaviors began at a certain time in the individual's life or they occur during only specific times of each day.

If the history of these behaviors relates to a situational crisis or loss, consider depression as the possible cause (e.g., "John was never described as hyperactive until his parents separated" or "Mary has become inattentive in class since her parents began openly fighting at home"). These behaviors might occur after such obvious stresses as parental fighting, separation, divorce, or the death of a family member. They might also occur after the birth of a sibling, moving to a new house, or starting a new school. The history of these behaviors has a discernible starting point and appears to be related to a life stress.

If the behaviors began after entering a particular environment, consider the environment. If the student has a learning disability and/or a sensory integrative disorder, or if one of these disorders is suspected, clarify whether they exist comprehensively before concluding that the diagnosis is ADHD. These disorders, their clinical symptoms, and the diagnostic process are discussed in Chapter 4.

If these behaviors are *chronic* and *pervasive* (chronic, in that they have been there forever; pervasive, in that they are there all of the time) consider ADHD.

Chronicity. Parents might report that their child's teacher complained that he could not sit still or pay attention in his fourth grade class and then add, "You think she has trouble, you should have heard his third grade teacher, and his second grade teacher, and his first grade teacher, and his kindergarten teacher. I have the only son who was kicked out of nursery school because he would not sit still during circle time and pay attention." Or a mother might report that her child kicked excessively in utero, squirmed in her arms, and has always been in motion. She might say, "He started to walk at 10 months, and from 10 months 1 second on, he would run into another room, out the door, or into the street if I was not there to stop him." She might then comment, "I can't remember one time in his whole life when he sat in his seat for the entire meal." It is evident by these observations that the behaviors have been present throughout the child's life.

Pervasiveness. The parents describe the hyperactivity, distractibility, and/or impulsivity. The classroom teacher also describes these behaviors as does the art, music, physical education teacher, and the lunch-room monitor. The Sunday School teacher, scout leader, or tutor sees the same behaviors. The behaviors are there all of the time.

Summary

All children and adolescents who show the behaviors of hyperactivity, distractibility, and/or impulsivity do not have ADHD. In reality, ADHD might be the *least* common cause for these behaviors. A clear differential diagnostic process that takes into account all possible causes for these behaviors is needed before a diagnosis is made.

Once the diagnosis is established, it is important to explore the impact of the disorder on the child or adolescent as well as on the family. ADHD behaviors will interfere with school performance. They will also interfere with family interactions and activities as well as with peer relationships and activities. The treatment plan must take into account the total child or adolescent in his or her total environment. It must go beyond prescribing medication.

It is also important to clarify whether the individual with ADHD also has a learning disability. If present, this disability must also be treated. The treatment for ADHD will not treat the learning disability, nor will the treatment for a learning disability treat the ADHD. They are associated, but are still different disorders.

If there are emotional, social, or family problems, the clinician must try to understand the role the ADHD plus possible learning disabilities might play in causing or contributing to these problems. The treatment plan will vary depending on whether the emotional, social, and/or family problems are seen as the primary difficulty or as secondary to the ADHD plus possible learning disabilities.

ASSOCIATED DISORDERS

Chapter 4

Learning Disabilities

As discussed throughout this book, individuals with attention-deficit hyperactivity disorder (ADHD) may also have a learning disability. In addition, children and adolescents with a learning disability can show behaviors suggestive of ADHD. Therefore, it is important for the clinician to understand learning disabilities.

A common clinical history heard by a health or a mental health clinician might go like this:

> A boy starts school and does not do well. By third grade he has not mastered basic skills and is held back in school. He is now a head taller and a year older than his classmates. His friends from the previous year move on and tease him about being kept back.
>
> By fifth grade, he is so far behind that he becomes increasingly frustrated, scared, and angry. He begins to act out in class. During these same years, his parents are also frustrated and worried and feel helpless. The school staff call constantly to complain of his behavior or his incomplete class work or homework.
>
> The parents' opinions on the situation differ increasingly. One believes that the best way to raise this child is to be firm and strict. The other believes that they should be understanding and permissive. Soon there are marital stresses.
>
> Finally, the principal meets with the parents and tells them that their son is emotionally disturbed, probably because of the marital problems. A referral to a child and adolescent psychiatrist or to another mental health professional is recommended.

In such cases, the clinician must sort out the cause from the consequence. Is the principal correct or might this boy have a learning disability? Might he have ADHD? Or might he have all of the above? If so, which came first and which is the consequence of the other (i.e., are the emotional and family problems causing the academic difficulties, or are the emotional and family problems a consequence of the academic disabilities)? Each conclusion leads to a very different treatment plan. The above questions can only be answered with a knowledge of ADHD and of learning disabilities. This chapter focuses on the question of learning disabilities.

What Are Learning Disabilities?
(The Formal Definition)

Public schools use the definition established by Federal law: Education for All Handicapped Children (Public Law 94-142). This definition uses inclusionary and exclusionary criteria to define learning disabilities:

> "Specific learning disabilities" means a disorder in one or more of the basic psychological processes involved in understanding or in using language, spoken or written, which may manifest itself in an imperfect ability to listen, think, speak, read, write, spell, or to do mathematical calculations. The term includes such conditions as perceptual handicaps, brain injury, minimal brain dysfunction, dyslexia, and developmental aphasia. The term does not include children who have learning problems which are primarily the result of visual, hearing, or motor handicaps, of mental retardation, of emotional disturbance, or of environmental, cultural, or economic disadvantage.

DSM-III did not reflect the educational approach used in this public law. Rather than focus on the underlying learning disabilities, DSM-III focused on the areas of academic difficulty, using the term *specific developmental disorders*. The specific subcategories focused on general areas of difficulty. The focus on being a developmental disorder reflected the fact that these disorders were found in children and adolescents and that they impacted significantly on all aspects of development. This term does not reflect the reality that for most, these disabilities will last throughout their lives.

DSM-III-R maintains the focus on specific developmental disorders and on general areas of difficulty. However, the subgroups are different than in DSM-III. Specifically:

- Academic skills disorders
    Developmental arithmetic disorder
    Developmental expressive writing disorder
    Developmental reading disorder
- Language and speech disorders
    Developmental articulation disorder
    Developmental expressive language disorder
    Developmental receptive language disorder
- Motor skills disorder
    Developmental coordination disorder

These specific developmental disorders are coded on Axis II. They are characterized by an inadequate development of specific academic, language, speech, and motor skills that are not due to demonstrable physical or neurological disorders, a pervasive developmental disorder, mental retardation, or deficient educational opportunities.

DSM-III-R differs significantly from federal and state classification systems for children and adolescents with learning disabilities. The latter systems state in their definition that such individuals are of at least average intelligence. In DSM-III-R, children who are performing academic skills below their intellectual potential are diagnosed as having an academic skills disorder even if they are mentally retarded.

The inclusion of these categories in a classification of "mental disorders" is considered controversial by some since many of the children with these disorders have no signs of psychopathology. Further, the detection and treatment of many of these disorders usually take place within schools rather than within the health or mental health systems. However, these conditions are strongly associated with primary (Axis I) disorders and conform to the DSM-III-R concept of a mental disorder (i.e., a mental disorder is conceptualized as a clinically significant behavioral or psychological syndrome or pattern that occurs in a person and that is associated with present distress or disability or with a significant increase in risk of suffering death, pain, disability, or an important loss of freedom).

When working in or with a school system, the term *learning disabilities* is used. When completing medical or insurance forms, the DSM-III-R term is used. Regardless of the label, the primary concern must be in an awareness of such a disability.

What Are Learning Disabilities?
(The Clinical Definition)

Most educational test instruments and special educational literature use a computer-based or cybernetics model for understanding learning and learning disabilities. It is understood that any learning task involves more than one process and that any learning disability can involve more than one area of dysfunction. However, breaking down the learning process into steps helps to clarify the process.

The first step in this model is *input*, where information from the sense organs is entered into the brain. Once the information is recorded, what is received is processed and interpreted, a process called *integration*. Next, the information must be used or stored and later retrieved, a process called *memory*. Finally, this information must be sent out through language or muscle activities, the *output* process. It is important to understand this input→integration→memory→output process and the terminology and concepts used by professionals in the field of learning disabilities.

Input Disabilities

Input is a central brain process and does not pertain to peripheral visual or auditory problems. This process of perceiving one's environment is referred to as "perception." A child might have a visual or an auditory perception disability.

Visual perception disability. Children with this disability may have difficulty in organizing the position and shape of what they see. Input may be perceived with letters reversed or rotated: an *n* might look like a *u*; an *E* might look like a *3*, *W*, or an *M*. The letters *d, b, p,* and *q* might be confused with each other. This confusion with position of input is normal until about age 5 or 6. The disorder becomes apparent when the child begins to copy letters or designs or to read or write.

Other children may have a "figure-ground" problem; that is, they have difficulty focusing on the primary figure rather than the visual inputs in the background. Reading requires this skill to focus on specific letters or groups of letters, then track from left to right, line after line. Children with this disability may skip over words, read the same line twice, or skip lines.

Judging distances or depth perception is another visual perception task that can be dysfunctional. Some children may misjudge depth, bumping into things, falling off a chair, or knocking over a drink because their hand reaches the glass sooner than expected.

Auditory perception disabilities. As with visual perception, children with this disability may have difficulty with one of several aspects of auditory perception. A child who has difficulty distinguishing subtle differences in sounds will misunderstand what is said and may respond incorrectly. Words that sound alike are often confused— "blue" with "blow," "ball" with "bell," or "can" with "can't." A boy is asked, "How are you?" and answers, "I'm 9-years-old." He thought he heard "old" instead of "are" or in addition to the "are."

Some children have difficulty with auditory figure-ground. For example, a child might be watching television in a room where others are playing or talking. A parent may call out to the child, and it might not be until the third verbalized paragraph that the child begins to pick the voice (figure) out of the other sound inputs (background). It seems that the child never listens or pays attention.

Finally, some children cannot process sound inputs as fast as normal people can. This problem is called an "auditory lag." At a normal rate of speech, the child needs to focus on each thought heard for a fraction of a second longer than most people must to understand. Therefore, that child must concentrate on what was just heard while trying to hold on to what is coming in next. Gradually, the child gets behind and must jump ahead to what is currently being said, so now part of what is being said is missed.

For example, a teacher explains a math problem. The child hears and understands steps one, two, and three then misses step four, picks up with step five and is lost and confused. Because of this disability, when parents and teachers talk to these children, it appears that they are not paying attention or not understanding what is being said.

Sensory integrative disorder. Several other sensory inputs are critical to function: tactile, proprioception, and vestibular. There is a debate whether these sensory input difficulties result in a learning disability. There is no debate that they interfere with awareness of the body and of body movement and are thus a life disability.

Children with *tactile* perception difficulties confuse input from the nerve endings in the skin for light touch and for deep touch (pressure). They may be tactically defensive. From early childhood, these children do not like being touched or held. They are sensitive to touch and may perceive it as uncomfortable. Often they complain of insignificant tactile stimulation: the tag on the back of a shirt, the belt being too tight, the clothes feeling funny. Parents learn that deep touch is tolerated better and may even be calming.

Some children with tactile sensitivity are defensive and try to avoid body contact. A child who reacts like this may be walking down the hall when another child lightly brushes against him or her. The child might respond as if the touch was a major blow and react by hitting the other child. Other children may experience touch deprivation and the need for body contact. These children might walk around the room touching other children to the annoyance of the other children and the teacher.

Joint position, muscle tone, movement, and body position are perceived through *proprioception* perception. This information is used by the brain to hold a body upright or to hold, push, pull, and carry. Individuals having difficulty with this sensory input may be confused with their body in space and have difficulty with muscle tone and postural mechanisms; thus they will have difficulty maneuvering their bodies to keep from losing balance. They may have difficulty with motor planning and with the coordinated use of muscles in activities such as buttoning and tying. Some children with this disability experience a proprioception deprivation and might stomp their feet or bump into walls.

Unclear *vestibular* perception may make it difficult for a child or adolescent to interact with gravity and sense body movement in space, particularly changes in the position of the head. Vestibular perception gives information on the body placement in space (e.g., upside down or lying on stomach or on back) and movement (e.g., fast, slow, around, forward, and backward). Some individuals may experience vestibular deprivation and enjoy spinning in chairs or on swings.

Depending on which sensory systems are involved in the sensory integrative disorder, children and adolescents may have problems with tactile sensitivity, coordinating body movements, and adapting to the position of the body in space. In addition, they may have difficulty with motor planning; that is, the ability to easily direct their bodies to perform activities in a smooth, coordinated manner.

Taste and smell. No research has been done to explore if taste and smell inputs might be dysfunctional with children and adolescents who have a learning disability. Because there are difficulties with the other sensory systems, it is possible that these systems might also be involved.

I have had parents report that their child's taste is supersensitive. They may report that their child does not like certain foods because they "taste funny" or "feel funny in my mouth." Other parents report that their child smells things that they do not. These children seem to be very sensitive to smells or smell things differently.

Integration Disabilities

Once information enters the brain, it has to be understood. At least three steps are required to do this: *sequencing, abstraction,* and *organization.* The process of integrating input thus requires sequencing, abstraction, and organization abilities.

A child or adolescent might have a disability in one area or in all three areas. If the disability in sequencing relates to visual input, it is called a *visual-sequencing disability.* If the difficulty lies with auditory input, it is called an *auditory-sequencing disability.* So, too, the child might have difficulty with *visual abstraction* or with *auditory abstraction.* Organization difficulties usually involve all areas of input.

Sequencing disabilities. Children with such a disability might hear or read a story, but, in recounting it, start in the middle, go to the beginning, then shift to the end. Eventually the whole story comes out, but the sequence of events is inaccurate. They may have the same difficulty in writing. All of the information is written but in the wrong order. Or they may see the word "dog" and read it as "god." Spelling words with all of the right letters in the wrong order can also reflect this disability.

These children may have difficulty using a sequence of facts. They may be able to memorize a sequence, the days of the week or the months of the year, for example, but be unable to use single units out of the sequence correctly. Asked what comes after August, these children cannot answer spontaneously and must go back over the whole sequence, "January, February, March . . ." before they can answer. These children may know the alphabet but cannot use the dictionary without continuously starting at "a" and working up to the letter used.

Abstraction disabilities. Once information is recorded in the brain and placed in the right sequence, meaning must be inferred. Most children with learning disabilities have only minor difficulties in this area. Abstraction, the ability to derive the correct general meaning from a particular word or symbol, is a very basic intellectual task. If the disability in this area is too great, the child is apt to be functioning at a retarded level.

Some children, however, have more subtle problems with abstraction. For example, a teacher reads a story about a police officer to a group of second or third graders and then begins a discussion of police officers in general. The students are asked whether they know any men or women who are police officers in their neighborhood and, if so, what they do. Children with an abstraction disability may not be able to answer the question; they can only talk about the particular officer in the story and not about police officers in general. Older children might have difficulty understanding jokes, since a lot of humor is based on a play on words, which confuses them. Likewise, they might have difficulty with idioms or puns. These individuals often take what is said literally and may appear to be paranoid.

Organization disability. Once recorded, sequenced, and understood, information must be integrated with a constant flow of data and then related to previously learned information. Some children have difficulty pulling together multiple parts of information into a full or complete concept. A child may learn a series of facts but not be able to answer general questions that require using these facts. Such an individual's notes, reports, desk, and/or locker are unorganized. Work needed at home may be left in school; work needed at school may be forgotten at home. Individuals with this disorder may have difficulty organizing and planning time. Parents may report that their child's room is disorganized, as well.

Memory Disability

Once information is received, recorded in the brain, and integrated, it has to be stored so that it can be retrieved later from either short-term memory or long-term memory.

Short-term memory is the process of retaining information for a brief time while attending to or concentrating on it. For example, after calling the information operator for a long-distance phone number, most people can retain the 10 digits long enough to dial the phone number if it is done right away. However, if there is a distraction in the course of dialing, the number may be forgotten. *Long-term memory* is the process by which information is stored permanently. It has been repeated often enough to be retained and retrieved by thinking of it.

Most children with a memory disability have a short-term one. Like abstraction disability, a long-term memory disability interferes so much with functioning that children with this disability are more likely to be functioning as retarded. A child with a short-term memory problem may require many more repetitions to retain what the average child retains after a few repetitions. Yet, the same child usually has no problem with long-term memory, surprising parents with details from years ago.

A short-term memory disability can occur with information received visually, a *visual short-term memory disability*, or with information received auditorily, an *auditory short-term memory disability*. Often, the two are combined. For example, a child might review a spelling list one evening and know it well while concentrating on it, but in school the next day it is forgotten. Or a teacher might go over a math concept in class until it is understood, yet the child forgets how to do the problems at home that night. Some students stop midway through what they are saying and say, "Oh, forget it" or "Never mind" because they forgot what they were saying. They hide their short-term memory problem with such statements.

Some individuals describe having difficulty retaining what they read. This problem might be a reflection of a short-term memory disability. They read the first paragraph and understand it. They read the second paragraph and understand it. They read the third and fourth and other paragraphs and understand each. Yet, when they get to the end of the chapter, they have forgotten what they have read.

Output Disabilities

Information is expressed by means of words, language output, or through muscle activity such as writing, drawing, gesturing, and motor output. Some children and adolescents have a *language disability* or a *motor disability*.

Language disability. Two forms of language are used in communication: spontaneous language and demand language. Spontaneous language occurs in situations where a person initiates whatever is said. Here, the person has the opportunity of selecting the subject, organizing his or her thoughts, and finding the correct words before speaking. In a demand language situation, someone else sets up a circumstance in which the person must communicate by, for instance, asking a question. It is then necessary to simultaneously organize, find the right words, and speak.

Children with a language disability usually have no difficulty with spontaneous language. They may, however, have problems with demand language. The inconsistency can be quite striking. A child may initiate all sorts of conversation, may never keep quiet, in fact, and may sound quite normal. However, put into a situation that demands a response, that same child might answer, "Huh?" or "What?" or "I don't know." The child may ask for the question to be repeated to gain time or may not answer at all. If the child is forced to answer, the response may be so confusing or circumstantial that it is difficult to follow, sounding totally unlike the child who was speaking so fluently just a moment ago.

Motor disabilities. Difficulty coordinating groups of large muscles such as the limbs or trunk is called a *gross motor disability*. Difficulty performing tasks that require the coordination of groups of small muscles is called a *fine motor disability*.

Gross motor disabilities may cause the child to be clumsy, stumble, fall, bump into things, or have difficulty with generalized physical activities like running, climbing, or swimming. The child might have difficulty with buttoning, zipping, or typing.

The most common form of a fine motor disability is writing. The problem lies in part in an inability to get the many small muscles in the dominant hand to work together as a team. Children with this "written language" disability have slow, difficult to perform, poor handwriting. They complain that "their hand does not work as fast as their head is thinking." In addition to the mechanical aspect of writing, these children may have difficulty with the flow of thoughts through the muscles onto the page. They might make spelling, grammar, or punctuation errors or write with poor syntax.

If the child has a visual perception disability and thus provides incorrect information for the brain to use in doing motor tasks, there will be eye-hand coordination difficulties. For example, the child might have difficulty coloring and staying in the line, cutting and staying on the line, or catching a ball. These difficulties are called *visual motor disabilities.*

The Learning Disability Profile

Obviously, the learning process is much more complex. However, this simple model for describing specific learning disabilities can be helpful. Individuals with a learning disability will have a profile of learning abilities and learning disabilities. There is no set pattern of learning disabilities. Each child and adolescent must be evaluated and understood individually. This evaluation is essential for understanding these children and adolescents and for planning the appropriate educational and/or clinical interventions.

Clinical Evidence Suggesting a Learning Disability

When a clinician evaluates a child or adolescent with emotional or behavioral problems that are associated with poor academic performance, he or she must consider the possibility of ADHD and/or of a learning disability, and gather information from every source available.

Parents can provide a history of school experiences, starting with preschool: Has the child had difficulty year after year? Have teachers described the child as hyperactive or distractible in each grade? Has the child had academic problems every year?

The child or adolescent can be of help, too. Knowing the input→integration→memory→output model, the clinician can ask questions about school performance. In this part of a "systems review," the clinician should start with the basic skills. The following questions can provide useful information.

Reading

- How well do you read? Do you like to read?
- When you read, do you make mistakes like skipping words or lines or reading the same lines twice?
- Do you find that you can read each line or paragraph but that when you finish the page or chapter you don't remember what you have read?

Writing

- How is your handwriting?
- Do you find that you cannot write as fast as you are

thinking? If so, do you overlap words because you are thinking of the next word but writing another?
* How is your spelling? Grammar? Punctuation?
* Do you have difficulty copying off of the blackboard?

Math

* Do you know your multiplication tables?
* When you do math do you make mistakes like write "21" when you meant to write "12," or do you mix up your columns or add when you meant to subtract?
* Do you sometimes start a math problem but halfway through forget what you are trying to do?

Other questions can focus on areas not covered under the review of specific skills.

Sequencing

* When you speak or write, do you sometimes have difficulty getting everything in the right order, that is do you start in the middle, go to the beginning, then jump to the end?
* Can you tell me the months of the year? Fine, now what comes after August? (Once answered, ask how he or she got the answer.)
* Do you have trouble using the alphabet in order?
* Do you have to start from the beginning each time?

Abstraction

* Do you understand jokes when your friends tell them?
* Do you sometimes get confused when people seem to say something yet they tell you they meant something else?

Organization

* What does your notebook look like?
* Is it a mess with papers in the wrong place or falling out?
* What about your desk? Your locker?
* Do you have difficulty organizing your thoughts or the facts you are learning into a whole concept so that you can learn it?
* Do you find that you can read a chapter and answer the

questions at the end of the chapter but that you are still not sure what the chapter is about?

- Do you have trouble planning your time so that things get done on time?
- What does your bedroom at home look like?

Memory

- Do you find that you can learn something at night and then go to school the next day and forget what you have learned?
- When talking, do you sometimes know what you want to say but halfway through you forget what you are saying? If so, do you cover up by saying things like, "Oh, forget it" or "It's not important"?

Language

- When the teacher is speaking in class, do you have trouble understanding or keeping up?
- Do you sometimes misunderstand people and, therefore, give the wrong answer?
- When people are talking, do you find that you have to concentrate so hard on what they say that you sometimes fall behind and have to skip quickly to what they are saying now to keep up?
- Does this sometimes cause you to get lost in class?
- Do you sometimes have trouble getting your thoughts organized when you speak?
- Do you have a problem finding the word you want to use?

Often, when I go over these questions with my patients they look amazed and ask me if I could read their mind. How could I have known about their problems? Sometimes, they did not understand their problems until they had to explain them to me.

During the diagnostic sessions, the clinician might pick up other clues of a learning disability. These children and adolescents may have difficulty with listening and understanding what the clinician says or with expressing themselves clearly. These individuals may have difficulty performing activities that require visual perception or visual motor tasks or playing a game that requires reading, counting, or following a sequence.

Learning disabilities are life disabilities; they do not just interfere with reading, writing, or math. They also interfere with baseball, basketball, four square, hopscotch, jump rope, dressing, setting the dinner table, and making small talk. The history from the parents or from the individual might provide clues from activities other than school that are suggestive of a learning disability. Using the input→integration→memory→output model, the discussion that follows illustrates such problems.

Learning Disabilities as Life Disabilities

Input disabilities. Children and adolescents with visual perception difficulties may have problems with sports that require catching, throwing, or hitting a ball. These motor tasks require visual figure-ground ability to spot the ball and depth-perception ability to track the ball, as well as visual motor ability to convert the input information into getting the body and arms to the right place at the right time.

Individuals with depth-perception problems may fall off of their seats, bump into things, and misjudge the distance to a drink and knock over the glass. Some may be confused by large, open spaces such as gyms or shopping malls. It is possible that some individuals with this problem might develop an anxiety disorder or panic disorder related to open spaces.

Individuals with an auditory perception problem might misunderstand what others say and thus respond incorrectly. Some may have difficulty knowing what sounds to listen to. They might miss what is being said to them by parents or friends because they were listening to one sound and did not realize that another sound had started. Some may have a delay in processing speech. They appear to be not listening or to be staring into space. They might be called an "air head" or "space cadet."

Less is known about other sensory inputs. Infants and children may be tactilely defensive, confused, or uncomfortable with touch. Some complain of clothes being too tight or of certain materials feeling uncomfortable. Some children seem hypersensitive to smell, complaining of things or places smelling funny. Others may have an oversensitive sense of taste.

We know little about the effect of perception problems during infancy. If such disabilities are apparent with young children, might they not have been present since birth? How would they impact on early interactions or on bonding if the infant misperceived sounds, visions, smells, or touch? Could these difficulties explain in part the frequent complaint by parents that their child had difficulty with eating, sleeping, and being calmed from the earliest weeks of life?

Integration disabilities. Children and adolescents with sequencing problems may confuse the steps involved in playing a game or might hit the ball and run to third base rather than first base. Young children might have difficulty dressing, putting on pants before the underpants. Such an individual might have difficulty following directions or making the bed, building models, or setting the dinner table properly.

Much of humor is based on subtle changes in the meaning of words or phrases. Individuals with difficulty with abstraction may miss the meaning of jokes and feel out of place with peers. They might have difficulty understanding slang expressions. Some will appear anxious because they misinterpret words or actions or interpret them more concretely.

Organizational problems may be reflected in a disorganized room or notebook or in an inability to plan time or to carry out activities. Parents and friends complain that such individuals can't get their act together.

Memory disabilities. Children and adolescents with this disability may meet someone they have known for a long time but not remember his or her name. Parents report that they cannot give more than one instruction at a time. They might ask their child to go to the garage and get the hammer, some nails, and a ruler, and the child returns with the hammer only. Also, for reasons explained above, some individuals can frustrate their parents and friends, because they stop in the middle of what they are saying and say, "Oh, forget it."

Output disabilities. The inability to write quickly and legibly or to spell can be problematic with games, activities, taking telephone messages, or writing a note to a friend. Mistakes are laughed at or associated with not being smart. Motor coordination difficulties can cause problems with buttoning, tying, zipping, playing games, cutting up food, or sports. Since success in sports is such a major part of childhood peer acceptance, difficulties with motor coordination can be a major social handicap.

Expressive language problems make communication difficult with peers, siblings, and adults. Individuals with this disability will have problems with small talk or with interacting in a conversation. Often they are shy and avoid talking or being with people for fear that they will say the wrong thing and appear foolish.

Establishing the Diagnosis of a Learning Disability

If the clinician determines—based on the medical evaluation, the family and school history, and the clinical and observational data—that there is a possibility of a learning disability, a referral should be made to confirm the diagnosis. The diagnosis is confirmed through psychological and educational testing. These studies might be done by one person or by a diagnostic team. This "psychoeducational" evaluation assesses three areas: 1) the individual's intellectual potential and cognitive style, 2) the individual's level of academic skills, and 3) evidence of a specific learning disability.

The psychological assessment may consist of a neuropsychological or a clinical-psychological evaluation. IQ test results are an important aid, especially in indicating whether there are any discrepancies between the verbal and performance IQ scores or between individual subtest scores on formal tests of intellectual assessment. Other psychological tests will assess perception, cognitive, and language abilities. The educational diagnostician or the psychologist will measure the individual's current level of academic skills using standard achievement tests. If, after these studies, there is a suggestion of a learning disability, the individual will be evaluated further for the presence of learning disabilities using specific tests (e.g., the Woodcock-Johnson Psychoeducational Battery).

If the disabilities are in the motor areas, an occupational therapist will be needed to perform further studies. If the disabilities are in the language areas, a speech and language therapist should do an assessment. Other professionals might be part of the diagnostic team if the initial studies suggest other specific problem areas (e.g., audiology and neurology).

The results of these evaluations should establish the presence or absence of a learning disability. If present, the results will also clarify the specific areas of the learning disability and of learning abilities.

Treatment for Learning Disabilities

The treatment of choice for learning disabilities in school is special education. Professionals trained in the area of learning disabilities work on overcoming the learning disabilities and on helping the individual compensate for those disabilities that cannot be overcome. Strategies for learning are taught based on the individual's areas of strengths and weaknesses; the classroom teacher must learn to build on the individual's strengths in the classroom while helping to accommodate for the weaknesses.

The treatment of choice for learning disabilities outside of school is educating the parents and their child. They all must learn to build on strengths while understanding and adapting to or accommodating for the weaknesses. The parents must use this knowledge to select chores or activities or sports or camps where their child will most likely find success.

My book, *The Misunderstood Child, A Guide for Parents of Learning Disabled Children* (McGraw-Hill, 1984) expands on these concepts. It is written primarily for parents and discusses how they can build on their child's strengths rather than magnify his or her weaknesses as they try to help their child and their family.

Summary

Learning disabilities and ADHD are related but different disorders. Children who cannot sit still or who are distractible and who cannot stay on task will have difficulty learning. It is important to differentiate if the individual has ADHD, a learning disability, or both.

It is also important to suspect a learning disability with any individual referred due to school, academic, and behavioral problems. Children and adolescents with learning difficulties only will be referred for a psychoeducational evaluation. Children and adolescents with behavioral or emotional problems will be referred to the family physician, pediatrician, child/adolescent psychiatrist, or another mental health professional. Each professional must look for the possibility of ADHD as well as for the possibility of a learning disability. If there are emotional or behavioral problems, the clinician must determine if they are the cause of the academic difficulties or if they are the consequence of the academic difficulties.

Treatment interventions should be based on the diagnostic profile. The treatment for a learning disability will not treat ADHD nor will the treatment for ADHD treat a learning disability. A primary focus on the emotional or behavioral problems without addressing the underlying causes for these problems will be less than successful.

Chapter 5

Associated Emotional, Social, and Family Problems

When parents contact a health or mental health professional, they often present problems relating to their child's behavior. It is critical for the professional to assess whether the behavioral difficulties are the primary theme or whether they are reflective of another disorder. The following case example illustrates this.

Case example

Mrs. Smith called, requesting that I see her 9-year-old son Bobby. He had just been suspended from fourth grade because of fighting. Over the telephone she commented that he has been a problem most of his life.

Mr. and Mrs. Smith were seen initially. Mrs. Smith reported that the pregnancy and delivery were without problems. She brought Bobby home from the hospital on the third day. The first 3 months were described as impossible. He had colic, and feeding him was difficult. The pediatrician tried several milk formulas, finally finding a soy-based one that seemed to help. Bobby would sleep for only 2 hours and then wake up crying; he did not sleep through the night until he was 10 months old. His parents recalled these months as a "living hell" because nothing seemed to comfort him.

Bobby's motor and language development were appropriate for his age. Mr. Smith recalled that Bobby started to walk at 10 months and that "at 10 months and 1 minute you had to chase him or he would run out of the house." They reported no other problems until Bobby was 2 years old. Toilet training was difficult. He was finally bowel trained by age 2 years, 10 months. He remains enuretic.

Bobby entered a part-time nursery school at age 3. The staff suggested that he was not ready for school. They described him as running all over the room, not paying attention to the group, and hitting other children. His parents reported similar behavior at home. He was always on the move. They could not get him to sit in their lap and listen to a story. He had a "short fuse" and cried or hit if he was not able to get what he wanted or if his sister, who was 2 years older, made him unhappy.

Bobby was placed in nursery school again when he was 4 years old. He had difficulty throughout the year. The teachers complained that he would not sit still during circle time nor would he pay attention during group activities. Often, he would get up and wander about the room. If another child did not do what he wanted he would hit the child.

There was no improvement in kindergarten. Bobby's parents did report some improvement in first grade. He had a firm but caring teacher who stayed on top of him. She also allowed him to walk around. Second grade was not good. The teacher complained about his inability to stay seated and his constant fidgeting. Each report card noted that he could do so much better if he would just stay on task and complete his work. Bobby would occasionally get into trouble with the other children during unstructured times like recess. There was no improvement in third grade.

Bobby started fourth grade promising his parents that he would be a good boy this year. By the end of October, his parents were called in for a conference. Bobby was constantly moving about the room and bothering the other children. Even when he worked at his desk, he would distract the other children by tapping his pencil or playing with his books. The teacher viewed him as immature because he would not stay on task and complete his work unless she worked with him. The other children seemed to not like him and often teased him. Bobby's parents were asked to talk to him to get him to understand that he was now in fourth grade and had to grow up.

In late December Bobby hit a boy who teased him. This boy's mother called to complain, and Bobby was suspended from school for 3 days. The principal told his parents that they needed to get help for Bobby before he "grew up to be a delinquent."

When questioned, Bobby's parents agreed that he had been active and fidgety all of his life. They, too, could see that he had a difficult time paying attention. Whether they were reading to him, he was playing with his toys, or he was doing homework, Bobby was constantly distracted by other activities. He always had a short temper, striking out or having a tantrum if frustrated. In addition, they reported that he stole money from them. Since he was their first boy, they had assumed that boys were just different than girls.

When Bobby was seen, he presented as a delightful, pleasant boy. During the evaluation sessions, he was not active and he did not appear to be distractible. His choice of play activity, play, interactions, and fantasy appeared to be age-appropriate. After the second session, I wondered why my observations did not match the history given by his parents.

With the parents' permission, I spoke to Bobby's teachers and to his scout leader. Each described his hyperactivity, distractibility, and impulsivity. I had to conclude that my office was quiet and had few distractions. He had no academic demands, and he received one-on-one attention from me. The in vivo descriptions by the others were more valid in assessing him for

hyperactivity, distractibility, or impulsivity than my office observations.

   At the time of the evaluation, Bobby was not functioning well
in school. He had poor peer relationships, and his at-home behavior resulted in constant yelling, fighting, and punishment.
Both his teachers and parents felt overwhelmed and helpless.

This clinical case is not unique. The common theme is a chronic
and pervasive history of hyperactivity, distractibility, and impulsivity.
The early history of difficulty with eating, sleeping, and irritability is
not uncommon among children with attention-deficit hyperactivity
disorder (ADHD). Year after year the teachers correctly identified the
behaviors, yet no one recognized the probable cause. Each projected
his or her frustration and anger onto the child and parents. By the
time Bobby came to see me there were emotional, social, and family
problems. However, these problems were secondary to an unrecognized and untreated disorder and were not the primary disorder. If
individual and family psychological interventions had been initiated,
he might have improved for short periods of time but the hyperactivity, distractibility, and impulsivity would have persisted. By treating
the ADHD in addition to providing the needed individual and family
help, the total clinical picture could be improved.

   ADHD is a presumed neurologically based disorder. The case of
Bobby suggests that the disorder had probably been present since
birth and that the behaviors were apparent from the earliest years.
ADHD is not a school disability. It is a life disability. The same behaviors of hyperactivity, distractibility, and/or impulsivity that interfere
with school availability and performance interfere with family life and
peer relationships. It is not uncommon to develop emotional, social,
and family problems. It is critical that the clinician recognize the
ADHD if it is present and understand the impact this disorder can
have on the individual.

Emotional and Behavioral Problems

As discussed in Chapter 2, referral bias results in the misdiagnosis of
many children and adolescents with ADHD as emotionally disturbed.
In addition, some individuals with ADHD are not recognized or diagnosed. Children and adolescents who are hyperactive and/or impulsive are more likely to be recognized; thus they are more likely to be
referred for diagnosis and treatment. Those who may be only distractible are often missed. These individuals are frustrated and may have
academic difficulties; however, they do not disrupt the class and thus
do not get referred for evaluation. Girls who are only distractible ap-

pear to be the group of ADHD children and adolescents most often missed. For cultural reasons, they are less likely than boys are to act out their frustration.

When observing the behavioral or emotional problems associated with ADHD, it is helpful to note the specific behaviors of hyperactivity, distractibility, and impulsivity and how each can impact on life tasks as well as on family, peer, and school relationships. These behaviors can result in difficulty mastering each stage of psychosocial development. The presenting behavioral or emotional problems might reflect clinical evidence of many diagnoses found in DSM-III-R. The critical issue for the clinician is to be aware of ADHD when evaluating children and adolescents with behavioral and emotional problems.

The behaviors associated with ADHD create stress in all aspects of psychosocial development. How these behaviors impact on the psychosocial functioning of the individual and how they are expressed are influenced by the individual's culture, age, and sex, as well as by the family, school, and community acceptance of these behaviors. Each individual will develop a specific repertoire of resulting behaviors, developing coping strategies or becoming dysfunctional.

If the hyperactivity, distractibility, and/or impulsivity are not recognized year after year, these individuals may externalize their frustration by getting angry, losing their tempers, or hitting. The feelings might be internalized, resulting in a poor self-image (as a bad person), sadness, and possibly in depression. These feelings might be magnified by the teacher's and parents' frustration. They may tell these children that they are bad or that their behaviors are done on purpose.

As discussed in Chapter 3, children and adolescents with ADHD manifested by hyperactivity and/or impulsivity often develop an oppositional defiant disorder or a conduct disorder. The reason for this frequent relationship is not known. One possible explanation is that there is a common neurological theme with ADHD and these disruptive behavioral disorders. Another possibility is that these behaviors statistically coexist (i.e., comorbidity) to a greater extent than would be expected.

Social Problems

Children and adolescents with ADHD often do not relate well to peers and may not be accepted by these peers. These problems can occur with classmates and neighbors. Difficulties can be found in out-of-school activities such as scouts, organized sports, and religious education. This peer rejection can be devastating and can result in feelings of loneliness, a poor self-image, and low self-esteem. As adolescents, such problems and feelings can lead to poor school performance, juvenile delinquency, and dropping out of school. Research has shown that the longer-term outcome for children without positive peer relationships can include occupational difficulties, alcoholism, significant psychiatric disorders, and antisocial behaviors.

The behaviors associated with ADHD can result in social problems. It is not uncommon for parents and teachers to complain that the child or adolescent has few or no friends, cannot keep friends, or relates poorly to peers. The hyperactivity and distractibility can be annoying but tolerated. The impulsivity is less well accepted.

In addition, some children and adolescents feel so out of control that they take extra measures to be in control. When with peers, they may be bossy and demanding. Frustration may result in anger, and anger in a child who is impulsive can result in aggressive behaviors. Adolescents may annoy their friends with their constant activity or with their inability to pay attention.

Many children and adolescents with ADHD show difficulty with social skills and awareness of social cues. They do not recognize the tone of voice or the body language that suggests their behavior is annoying someone. They may have only limited age-appropriate social skills needed to interact in a positive way with peers. If they are impulsive, each of these problems is made worse. They not only misinterpret social situations, they often act and speak before they think, resulting in behaviors that annoy or anger peers and lead to peer rejection.

All of these problems are seen in the classroom, in the halls, and on the playground. Each of the behaviors causes problems. For example, a student may be disruptive in the classroom, be inattentive, and require frequent comments from the teacher to return to the task to be done. This student may be verbally intrusive, interrupting the teacher or other students. The student's increased activity level, vocalizations, increased contacts with classmates, and frequent fidgeting impact negatively on teachers and on other students.

Often, students with ADHD have academic difficulties. Each of the behaviors associated with ADHD can interfere with success in school. Attentional difficulties may result in experiencing difficulty sustaining attention and being easily distractible. Work may be incomplete or not finished on time. Impulsivity may result in rushing through work or writing the first thought that comes to mind. This lack of reflectivity may result in frequent erasures and errors, careless mistakes, and incorrect work. The final result for such students may be performances below their abilities and possible failure. The combination of annoying behaviors in the classroom, frequent corrections by the teacher, and poor academic performance may lead to the other students viewing them as dumb, thus contributing to peer rejection.

Family Problems

When someone in the family is hurting, everyone feels the pain. Children and adolescents with ADHD can be difficult to live with and/or to manage. Parents feel the stress, as do the siblings. The hyperactivity, distractibility, and/or impulsivity can result in disruptive or dysfunctional behaviors. Furthermore, studies show that parents and siblings of ADHD children are more likely to experience their own psychological distress and psychiatric disorders than are those of normal children.

The Child

Many children with ADHD are difficult from birth. They may have irregular rhythms; poor adaptability; withdrawal, rather than approach, behaviors; high energy levels; and high irritability. As a result, they might have eating problems, require little sleep, and be difficult to comfort. With each year they become more and more different and difficult to parent.

As these children grow older, the eating and sleeping problems might resolve; however, the parenting problems continue. Soon, sibling conflicts begin. Preschool and regular school teachers may complain to the parents of their child's behavior. Difficulties develop with friends. Baby-sitters come once but not again. A simple trip to the supermarket becomes a crisis as the ADHD child runs up and down the aisles or has a tantrum when the parent refuses to purchase something. Parents feel frustrated and helpless. They try many models of discipline but none seem to work. The family doctor often says, "Don't worry about it . . . he'll outgrow it." But he doesn't.

Soon the parents might disagree on the best approach for helping. One feels that they should be more firm and strict; the other feels that they should be more understanding and permissive. Marital stress might begin. Home life becomes such a stress that one parent finds reasons to go out at night or to remain at work later.

Likewise, the siblings may become upset. They do not like to live in this environment and are jealous of the extra attention this child receives. They may become angry at the double standard—when the child with ADHD does something wrong it is sometimes overlooked; when they do the same thing they are punished. They also must deal with embarrassment, for example, when the child with ADHD comes into their room and takes things or gets frustrated and breaks things or has a tantrum when their friends are around.

It is essential to recognize the familial stresses on children and adolescents with ADHD, the parents, and the siblings. Because everyone in the family is hurting, the needs of each must be addressed.

The Parents

Parents may be at risk of experiencing excessive stress for two reasons. First, it is a challenge to raise a child with ADHD. Second, because there is a hereditary predisposition to this disorder, these parents have a higher rate of ADHD and psychiatric problems than those in the general population. Studies show that up to 20% of mothers and up to 30% of fathers of children with ADHD also have ADHD. There is also a greater chance of ADHD among the biological siblings of ADHD children; 30 to 35% may have ADHD.

Parents of children and adolescents with ADHD experience greater stress in their role as caretakers of these children, lower levels of self-esteem, higher levels of depression, more self-blame, and greater social isolation than do parents of normal children. Hence, the possibility of marital stress is higher in families with children who have ADHD.

Parents of children with ADHD are more likely to experience a variety of psychiatric disorders than are parents of normal children. These psychiatric disorders, reported in research literature, include conduct problems and antisocial behavior, alcoholism, affective disorders, and learning disabilities. It is unclear if these problems are a reflection of the stress involved in raising a child with ADHD, a reflection of the parent's ADHD plus possible learning disabilities, or a reflection of a broader genetically based biological vulnerability. For example, if the mother of a child with ADHD is alcohol dependent, is this alcoholism an effort to self-medicate her own hyperactivity, handle the stresses related to child care, handle the stresses of her own unrecognized and untreated ADHD plus possible learning disabilities and the resulting low self-esteem and career underachievement, or is it a result of a biological predisposition to substance abuse?

Several studies have shown a greater incidence of antisocial behavior and alcoholism among first-degree relatives of children with ADHD. Furthermore, the children with ADHD who had first-degree relatives with antisocial behavior or alcoholism were more likely themselves to have or have had conduct problems and antisocial behavior than were other children with ADHD. Children with ADHD who did not have these behavioral problems often had a greater history of associated learning disabilities among their relatives. These studies concluded that family histories of alcoholism and antisocial behavior are associated only with antisocial behavior in children and not with ADHD.

One way of understanding these observations and studies is to see the behaviors and psychiatric difficulties of parents of children with ADHD as reflecting several possibilities. For some, the problems reflect the stress of raising a child or adolescent with ADHD. For others, the problems might reflect this stress as well as be a consequence of the parent also having had ADHD plus a possible learning disability. If neither disorder was identified or treated, or if they were identified but poorly or incompletely treated, the adult may show the consequences of these disorders. For yet others, the problems might not only reflect unrecognized and untreated or poorly treated ADHD plus a possible learning disability but might also reflect that these disorders still exist and still impact on the parent. To add to the complication, I have worked with some families in which the parents were also reflecting the consequence of having had parents who appear to have had ADHD, thus impacting on their childhood.

Summary

If a child or adolescent is diagnosed as having ADHD, the associated emotional, social, and family problems must be recognized and identified. The treatment plan must address these problems as well as the ADHD. Such treatment approaches are discussed in Chapters 7 through 10.

The critical question for the clinician is whether the emotional, social, and family problems are causing the hyperactivity, distractibility, and/or impulsivity or whether the emotional, social, and family problems are a consequence of ADHD. Each conclusion leads to a different understanding and a different treatment plan.

ETIOLOGY OF ATTENTION-DEFICIT HYPERACTIVITY DISORDER

Chapter 6

Etiology of Attention-Deficit Hyperactivity Disorder

Any discussion on the etiology of attention-deficit hyperactivity disorder (ADHD) must be considered as reflective only of our current state of knowledge. It is difficult to use much of the previous research data and some of the current research studies because there is a lack of diagnostic criteria agreed on by all researchers. In addition, many studies were done prior to the formulation of the diagnostic criteria found in DSM-III and DSM-III-R. Some earlier studies examined hyperactivity only because it was the primary behavior noted in DSM-II. Other earlier studies used the criteria for Minimal Brain Dysfunction and combined learning problems, hyperactivity, distractibility, and behavioral problems.

Another reason it is difficult to review all aspects of the etiology relating to ADHD is that there are many factors related to attention. Current research supports this view. Thus, there are a group of attentional disorders of which ADHD may be but one clinical type.

The current view is that there is a biological-neurological etiology for ADHD and that how it is manifested is influenced by psychological and social factors. It is the interaction of both influences that explain the clinical picture.

For example, the way an individual will express the frustration caused by ADHD will be influenced by culture and sex. A girl with distractibility who is doing poorly in school and feeling frustrated might withdraw and appear disinterested or depressed. A boy with the same problems might misbehave and get into trouble. Each has ADHD. The boy is more likely than the girl is to be recognized and diagnosed.

There is also evidence of a genetic factor. Some studies suggest that 30 to 40% of children and adolescents with ADHD have inherited a familial pattern. Most likely a parent, sibling, or other biological relative also has or had ADHD. This suggestive evidence of a genetic influence supports the neurochemical theories on the etiology of this disorder. Other studies have focused on other factors that might influence fetal development.

These genetic, neurochemical, and other factors will be discussed in detail since the rationale for the current treatment of ADHD with specific medications is based on a neurochemical theory.

Genetic Factors

Family studies, twin studies, and adoption and/or foster home studies suggest an important genetic contribution to ADHD. Family studies show an increased risk of ADHD in parents of second degree relatives of children diagnosed as having ADHD and in the siblings of boys with ADHD. Twin studies suggest a higher concordance rate for ADHD in monozygotic as compared to dizygotic twins. Foster children studies suggest an increased rate of ADHD in the biological parents of children with ADHD compared to that found either in the parents of normal children or in the adoptive, nonbiological parents of children with ADHD adopted at an early age.

The incidence of adoption of children and adolescents who have ADHD is about five times higher than the national norms for adoption. One could speculate about the parents of children placed for adoption or about the possible risk factors experienced during pregnancy and delivery; however, the reasons for such a high incidence are not known.

Neurochemical Factors

The compounds that have received the most attention as the possible cause of ADHD are the monoamines comprising the catecholamines (dopamine and norepinephrine) and the indoleamine, serotonin. The theories relate to factors in the development of these monoamines or in the breakdown process.

Briefly, catecholamines in the brain originate from the precursor amino acid L-tyrosine, which is transported to the brain via blood and concentrated within neurons. Dopamine formation proceeds via the enzyme tyrosine hydroxylase acting on tyrosine and resulting in the formation of L-dihydroxyphenylacetic acid (L-dopa), which is then decarboxylated to dopamine. Norepinephrine formation proceeds from dopamine via dopamine β-hydroxylase. Nerve stimulation or stimulation by drugs results in the release of a neurotransmitter into the synaptic cleft with subsequent inactivation by reuptake mechanisms and metabolism. The catecholamines are metabolized by two enzymes, monoamine oxidase and catechol methyltransferase. In the brain, the principal metabolite of dopamine is homovanillic acid; the principal metabolite of norepinephrine is 3-methoxy-4-hydroxyphenylglycol (MHPG), which in a series of metabolic steps analogous to those for the catecholamines forms serotonin. This is metabolized by monoamine oxidase to 5-hydroxyindoleacetic acid. Each of these chemicals can now be determined and measured in the urine, blood, or cerebrospinal fluid.

One suggestive line of evidence relating the monoamines to ADHD is the observation that stimulant medications produce a significant ameliorative effect on the behavioral symptoms. Evidence supports the probability that stimulant medications effect central catecholaminergic mechanisms. Stimulants act via central monoaminergic systems to inhibit reuptake, increase the release of amine, and inhibit monoamine oxidase activity. All are actions that serve to increase the concentration of either catecholamines, dopamine, or norepinephrine at the synaptic cleft. This commonality between the effects of stimulant medications on the behavioral symptoms of ADHD and their known mechanism of action suggests that brain catecholaminergic mechanisms could be influential in causing ADHD.

Evidence provided by examination of monoamines, their metabolites, and related enzymes in the blood, urine, and cerebrospinal fluid of children with ADHD as well as pharmacological studies support this monoamine theory. One suggestion is that the behaviors of ADHD may be caused by a deficiency of dopamine and/or norepinephrine, and that the stimulant medications decrease these behaviors by producing an increase in these monoamines.

To date there has been little evidence to suggest a role for serotonin in ADHD. No changes have been noted in the metabolic by-products of serotonin in the cerebrospinal fluid. Medications that impact on serotonin levels in the brain do not improve the behaviors of ADHD.

Fetal Development

Prenatal, natal, perinatal, and socioenvironmental factors may impact on the developing fetus. Examples of these are poor nutrition, absence of prenatal care, metabolic or toxic factors, infections, and stress. Each can result in prenatal difficulties, premature delivery, and/or low birth weight. Studies have shown a relationship between low birth weight and prematurity and hyperactivity, distractibility, and aggressive behaviors. Although not a firm correlation, some of the neurological findings with children who have ADHD suggest fetal distress, possibly during the third to fifth month of pregnancy.

In a large National Collaborative Perinatal Project that followed children from the diagnosis of pregnancy, the evaluations done at age

7 found suggestive correlations between those children with hyperactivity, a short-attention span, and impulsivity and the following prenatal factors: maternal cigarette smoking, convulsions during pregnancy, low fetal heart rate during the second stage of labor, lower placental weight, an increase in breech presentations, and increase in chorionitis.

Other prenatal stresses have been studied. Infections, metabolic disorders, exogenous toxins, and deficiency of diet can result in children who show a higher incidence of ADHD behaviors and/or those who evidence a learning disability. The correlations in these studies are less strong than those in the National Collaborative Perinatal Project studies.

More recent studies of substance abuse during pregnancy are distressing. Many of the babies of the women studied showed problems with hyperactivity, distractibility, and irritability. Although these children might meet the criteria for ADHD, their behaviors should be viewed as evidence of a more pervasive neurological disorder.

The above studies do not confirm cause and effect; however, they do provide important evidence supporting a role for prenatal influences in the development of ADHD. Possibly, in some cases it is the genetic code and in other cases it is one or more of these prenatal factors or others not yet clarified that result in ADHD.

Postnatal Factors

Studies on trauma during delivery or in later life do not show a clear correlation with ADHD. An increased incidence of learning and behavioral disorders is seen in children with seizure disorders, especially with epilepsy. However, it is not clear whether any specific behavioral disorder occurs more frequently than another or if the behavioral disorder is associated with the epilepsy.

Residual effects of viral encephalitis can include hyperactivity, distractibility, and/or impulsivity. Many children and adolescents who experience a closed head injury also display these same behaviors. Thus, it appears that pervasive trauma to the nervous system can result in ADHD or ADHD-like behaviors.

Environmental and Cultural Factors

Studies to date have not shown a relationship between ADHD and variables such as birth order, number of siblings, times moved, family income, mother's age, mother's educational level, or the father's educational level. The National Collaborative Perinatal Project did show suggestive evidence of environmental influences, although no correlation of cause and effect was noted. Children with ADHD were more likely to come from homes where the father was absent. Perhaps the manifestations of ADHD are related to adverse social conditions, primarily disruptive family relationships, or perhaps ADHD behaviors contribute to causing disruptive families.

Cultural influences may play a role. Activity level, loudness, attentiveness, and inappropriate behavior are considered as normal and acceptable or not normal or acceptable by different cultures. Thus, the same behaviors might be identified as a problem in some cultures and families and not in others.

The "Attentional Disorders"

Some researchers express concern with the concept of ADHD as defined in DSM-III-R. They believe that there are other reasons for attentional problems that are not reflected by the clinical disorder of ADHD. Research on the broader concepts of attentional problems focus on clarifying the process of attention in the brain and the multiple areas involved in this process.

Dr. Martha Denckla of Johns Hopkins University has attempted to expand the concept of ADHD by looking at the broad "executive functions" of the brain: planning and sequencing complex behaviors, paying attention to several components at once, grasping the gist of a complex situation, resisting distraction and interference, inhibiting inappropriate response tendencies, and sustaining behavioral output for relatively prolonged periods. She has noted that children with ADHD have areas of "executive dysfunction." Executive functions depend heavily on the integrity of the frontal lobes and their subcortical connections. In her studies, children with executive dysfunction have had problems planning, organizing, and managing time and space. She believes that it was the executive dysfunctions of children with ADHD that cause their academic failures. Her studies have focused on four areas: 1) the ability to focus attention, 2) the ability to plan ahead and organize information, 3) the ability to shift and be flexible in processing information, and 4) the ability to inhibit extraneous or unnecessary responses. Given Dr. Denckla's concepts, I suspect that ADHD relates to the first and/or fourth of these areas.

Dr. Alan Mirsky of the National Institute of Mental Health has studied the process of attention in the brain and the specific areas of the brain involved with each function. His research is based on a neuropsychological model of attention that assumed that information processing occurs in sequential fashion. He and his colleagues view attention as a complex process or set of processes. They are attempting to assign functional specialization of these components of attention to different brain regions, keeping in mind that some brain regions share more than one attentional function. Dr. Mirsky breaks attention down into a number of distinct functions: 1) the capacity to focus on or select some part of the environment, 2) the ability to sustain or maintain that focus for an appreciable period, and 3) the ability to shift adaptively from one aspect or element of the environment to another. Each behavior could be seen as part of the ADHD picture. Probably, the ability to sustain or maintain focus is most relevant to understanding attention.

Dr. M. Posner of the University of California, Los Angeles, has proposed a distributed neural system to account for the general properties of attention in human information processing. He and his colleagues have defined anterior and posterior attentional systems. (The posterior attentional system is considered to be a "bottom-up" system, involved in the representation and processing of sensation, whereas the anterior attentional system is considered to be a "top-down" system, involved in the representation and processing of action plans.) His research suggests that the posterior attentional system required to perform a visual orientation task is not dependent on a single area of the brain. Instead, attention in such a task may be dependent on several elementary attentional operations. He has suggested three functions: 1) disengagement, 2) movement, and 3) engagement of attention. His work suggests that the anterior attentional system may be related to the concept of sustained attention and thus to ADHD.

The research of Dr. James Swanson of the University of California, Irvine, and others suggests that children with ADHD have no difficulty with the posterior attentional system; that is, they can shift from one focus or task to another. However, there may be an abnormal functioning of the anterior attentional system, resulting in a failure to sustain focused attention.

At this time, the research on attentional disorders strongly suggests that the distractibility found in ADHD is secondary to an inability to sustain attention. These individuals appear to be able to seek and then focus on the necessary task then, when needed, shift focus to another task. However, they have difficulty sustaining attention while on task.

Summary

Current research supports an interactive model for the cause of ADHD, incorporating both biological and psychosocial factors. A child's genetic endowment or other prenatal, perinatal, or postnatal factors might provide the biological basis for these behaviors. However, the clinical expression of these behaviors is influenced considerably by the child's culture and environment.

Current and future research might clarify that there are a group of "attentional disorders" and that ADHD is only one type of such disorders. Until further clarified, the clinician can only address ADHD as described in DSM-III-R.

TREATMENT

Chapter 7

Basic Concepts in the Treatment of Attention-Deficit Hyperactivity Disorder

The treatment of attention-deficit hyperactivity disorder (ADHD) must be multimodal, including individual and family education, individual and family counseling, the use of appropriate behavior management programs, and the use of appropriate medications. This chapter focuses on the basic concepts in the treatment of ADHD. The following chapters address each aspect of this multimodal approach.

Because children and adolescents with ADHD have multiple areas of difficulty, it is necessary to use a multimodal approach. The total person must be understood in his or her total world. Each area of difficulty must be identified and addressed.

As discussed throughout this book, children and adolescents with ADHD often have a cluster of clinical difficulties: learning disabilities, Tourette's disorder, and secondary emotional, social, and family problems. It is ideal to be part of a multidisciplinary team that can assess the total individual and identify the areas of difficulty. If this is not possible, it is important that the primary clinician coordinate with the efforts of other professionals and the school system when ruling in or ruling out each disorder. In some cases the clinician might be able to speak to each professional involved in evaluating the individual and then try to summarize the full findings. In other situations, the clinician might only receive copies of the evaluations done by other professionals and will need to make an independent summary of the full assessment. It is important not to finalize the full diagnostic process or the comprehensive treatment plan until all available information is received and reviewed.

Individuals with a learning disability might become frustrated, anxious, or depressed, and these secondary emotional problems can lead to hyperactivity, distractibility, and/or impulsivity. If these individuals have learning disabilities and ADHD and the clinician only treats the ADHD, they may be able to sit still and be attentive in class, and the teacher will feel that they should be able to learn and keep up with the class. The learning disabilities may only now become obvious. If unrecognized, these children and adolescents may become anxious or depressed and, despite the successful treatment of the ADHD with medication, they once again might show behaviors of hyperactivity or distractibility in class. However, now these behaviors are due to the emotional consequences of not treating the learning disabilities and are not due to the ADHD. The clinician must continually consider all diagnostic possibilities during the treatment process.

At the risk of being perseverative, I must state again that if the individual has emotional, social, or family problems, it is critical to decide if these problems are *causing* the academic difficulties or if the emotional, social, and family problems are a *consequence* of the academic difficulties.

Treatment Planning

Once the data from the family, the school, and other professionals are collected and assessed, the full clinical picture will become apparent. A multimodal treatment plan can be developed to address each area of identified difficulty.

- If the individual has *ADHD*, educating and counseling the individual and family will be needed along with behavior management approaches, the use of the appropriate medication, and work with the school.
- If the individual has a *learning disability*, special-education therapy will be needed along with educating and counseling the individual and family and working with the school.
- If the individual has *secondary* emotional, social, and/or family problems, the primary disabilities (ADHD and possible learning disabilities) must be treated while implementing appropriate psychological interventions for the individual and family and working with the school.

Other interventions may be indicated, depending on the specific areas of difficulty found. Some of these interventions are done by health and/or mental health professionals whereas others are done by educational professionals (e.g., special educators, speech and language pathologists, and occupational therapists). In each case, the clinician must collaborate with these professionals while working with the child or adolescent and the family.

Summary

A multimodal treatment plan is necessary to treat ADHD. The clinician can be the director or coordinator of this plan or can be involved in one aspect of the plan. Whatever role the clinician plays, it is critical that all involved with the individual be aware of what the others are doing and that the efforts be coordinated. This multimodal treatment plan includes:
1. Individual and family education.
2. Individual and family counseling.
3. Appropriate behavior management programs.
4. Appropriate use of medication.

Chapter 8

Individual and Family Education

Much of the clinical picture seen at the time of assessment is confusing. The behaviors reflect possible attention-deficit hyperactivity disorder (ADHD) plus the possible associated disorders. Teachers might focus on the behaviors without recognizing the underlying disorders. They may describe the inability to sit still, stay on task, or complete a task or such impulsive behavior as interrupting or fighting. Parents might repeat the concerns of the school plus share their frustration and experiences. Often parents report that they have been talking to the teachers and to their family physician for years only to be told that they are "overworried parents" or that their child "will outgrow it." But, neither statement turned out to be true. The problems persisted and became worse.

The school staff, possibly because of their own frustration and feelings of helplessness, might displace these feelings onto the parents. Parents rarely, if ever, get a call from someone at the school saying, "Your child had such a great day, I would like to compliment you on being such a good parent." Instead, they receive calls telling them of their child's disruptive behaviors or of his or her incomplete work. The nonverbal message to the parents is, "Do something about it . . . make your child behave and learn."

Children and adolescents with ADHD also experience frustration. For them, also, the disabilities are invisible. They have had only one brain throughout their life and do not know that it is not functioning normally. All they know is that they want to be good; they want to be successful in school; they try as hard as the others; yet, they do not succeed and they seem to get into trouble. Over time they have been accused of being bad, lazy, or a troublemaker. Eventually they begin to identify themselves as such, and they begin to feel that they are dumber than their classmates or that they are bad.

The critical first step in any multimodal approach to treatment, therefore, must be to educate the parents and then their child. This educational process may be needed for other significant individuals such as siblings, grandparents, and child-care workers. Each must understand these invisible handicaps and must understand that, although invisible, these disabilities are just as debilitating as any other chronic handicapping condition. Each must understand that the individual with ADHD is not bad or dumb. Finally, each must understand the treatment plan.

In my practice, I have followed many individuals with ADHD from their childhood to their young adult life. Often, I ask them to tell me which interventions were most helpful over the years and which were not. I explain that I want to learn from them so that I can better help others. The most consistent response is, "When you first explained who I was." Before this time they saw themselves as dumb or bad. Afterwards, they began to understand their disabilities and, with this new insight, they were able to rethink and change their self-image.

As with any chronic illness, these children and adolescents must understand their disability and how it impacts on them during each stage of life. They also must understand the models of treatment, what the treatment is suppose to accomplish, and their critical role in this treatment program. By understanding and playing an active role in what happens to them, they will be more accepting of and compliant with the treatment programs.

Educational Process

The educational plan I use starts with my interpretive session with the parents. If their child has ADHD, I explain this disorder and the proposed treatment. (A model for the explanation is presented at the end of this chapter.) If the child has a learning disability, I explain what it is, using the input→integration→memory→output model described in Chapter 4. Before this session, I review the data from the psychoeducational evaluations. If I do not understand part of the report, I call the professional who did it and ask for help. I want to be able to translate the information into a form both I and the parents can understand. If there are emotional, social, and/or family problems, I discuss each and explain whether I see these problems as primary and causing the academic difficulties or secondary and a consequence of the ADHD and/or learning disabilities. I end the session by summarizing the necessary multimodal treatment plan, what role each has in the plan, and my specific role as part of the treatment team or as the coordinator of this team.

My second session is with the child. The same materials reviewed with the parents are reviewed with the child. The only difference for me between meeting with a 5 year old, a 10 year old, or a 15 year old is my communication style. I try to use information from the diagnostic sessions. For example, "You remember that you told me that when you read you often skipped words or lines. Well, that problem is because of the figure-ground difficulty we just discussed." When I describe the fidgetiness or the distractibility or the impulsivity, they know what I am talking about.

At the end of this session, I emphasize that they are not dumb or bad. I stress that now we know why they have had such difficulties in school and at home and that we can do many things to make their lives better and more successful. This last statement is critical. A clinician should never tell these individuals that they have a problem without immediately telling them how these problems will be addressed and helped.

My third session in this educational process is with the entire family. In addition to any siblings, I encourage other meaningful adults to attend. If there are grandparents who believe that there is nothing wrong with their grandchild and that the only problem is that the mother is not strict enough, I encourage them to come. The findings and the treatment recommendations are reviewed again. This time I try to get the child to help me. "Mary, I am not sure that I am doing a good job of explaining this problem to your brother. Can you think of an example that might help?" My goal is to educate each member of the family and to begin to change the role this child has played in the family. This individual is not the bad one of the family, the troublemaker in school, dumb, or retarded. There are reasons for the behaviors and problems, and something can be done to help. It is important, also, to support the parents and siblings. The behaviors they have had to endure should not be permitted to continue. They need to know that there were reasons for these behaviors, but that once the problems are addressed the behaviors are expected to decrease or stop. During this session, the clinician can get a better feel for the family dynamics and the types of family interventions that might be needed.

Some might feel that a three-session educational process is too lengthy. I find that these sessions are the most valuable. By the end of the last session, the parents, siblings, and the child with ADHD have more understanding of the nature of the problem and are less resistant to aiding in the resolution of the problems. I have given to them a knowledge base and built a relationship that can be used throughout the treatment process. Because ADHD plus possible learning disabilities may be chronic disorders, this treatment process may go on for years, being revised for each developmental stage. In the long run, these three sessions are a most clinically and time efficient use of effort.

Educational Process With the School

It is important that the school understand and accept the clinical findings. Teachers will need to know how to work most effectively with them. If medications are used, teachers and others will need to know what to observe and how to pass this information on to parents and clinicians.

Some school systems in this country encourage parents to see their family physician to establish the diagnosis of ADHD. After following these directions, parents sometimes return to the school to discuss their child's special needs, whereupon they are told, "Your child has a medical disorder and we have no responsibilities. The responsibilities are with your family physician." Yet, this child might need special education help for the ADHD or for an associated learning disability or secondary emotional or social problems.

The clinician must be willing to educate parents on their rights and on how to be an advocate for their child's needs. There are several support organizations listed at the end of this book (Appendix B) that can be helpful to these parents. The clinician might need to go to a meeting with the parents or to select someone else to go so the parents' and the child's needs are recognized and handled effectively.

Specific Education on the Use of Medication

The clinicians should only use medication when sure that the individual's behaviors are due to ADHD and, therefore, are neurologically based. If ADHD is diagnosed, the clinician must realize that this is a chronic and a pervasive disorder and must inform parents of two basic realities:

1. *ADHD is not a school disability. It is a life disability.* The brain does not know the difference between 9 A.M. and 6 P.M., Monday and Saturday, November and August, or school days and vacations. If the clinician only treats the individual's ADHD from 8 A.M. to 4 P.M. on school days, these individuals may do well at school. However, they will continue to have difficulty within the family, doing homework, and interacting with peers. The clinician must assess the need for medication during all hours of each day and use the medication for each period of time that it is needed.

2. *ADHD may persist beyond puberty, even into adulthood.* As discussed earlier, about 50% of children with ADHD will improve at puberty;

however, 50% will continue to have ADHD into adolescence. Of these, about 50% or more may continue to have ADHD as adults. There is nothing magical about puberty. Individuals that continue to have ADHD continue to need treatment.

It is important that the parents understand the concept of ADHD and the reasons for the proposed treatments. It is equally important for ADHD children and adolescents to understand. Many parents are fearful of medication. They do not want their child to be "drugged" or "sedated" or "tranquilized." It is important for them to understand that we do not use "drugs," we use "medications," and that these medications do not drug, sedate, or tranquilize their child. These medications allow the individual to function "normally" by presumably correcting a neurochemical deficit in the brain, which allows the brain to act normally. A model for explaining this concept is discussed later in this chapter.

Some parents have heard partial or incorrect information on some of the medications used. They might have read the *Physician's Desk Reference* and not realized that the Food and Drug Administration (FDA) requires that all side effects be listed, even those that are rare or that have been reported only a few times. The clinician must listen to the concerns and answer the questions. The information needed to do this is provided later in this chapter.

Much of the misinformation was provided to parents by the mass media during the summer of 1988. During the spring of 1988 a group called the Citizens Commission on Human Rights began to attack the use of Ritalin (methylphenidate hydrochloride). They circulated a small flyer entitled, "How Psychiatry Is Making Drug Addicts out of America's Children." As stated in the flyer, this organization was sponsored by the Church of Scientology, which has an extensive history of attacking the use of medications for the treatment of psychiatric disorders.

This group used a model that is not uncommon for the sponsoring organization. To gain media attention, they announced they were filing a class-action suit against the American Psychiatric Association, representing the group of physicians most commonly prescribing Ritalin, and CIBA-Geigy Pharmaceutical Company, representing the major manufacturer of Ritalin. This statement gained the Citizens Commission spokespersons air time on many of the national and local television and radio talk shows, and the print media followed up with interviews. In these interviews, the spokespersons could, and did, say anything to support their views. They offered few facts and often gave incorrect data; at times they gave "information" that was partially or completely incorrect. Unfortunately, many viewers assumed that if the person said it on television or radio, it had to be true.

In the fall of 1988, when media interest ceased, this group quietly announced to the American Psychiatric Association and to CIBA-Geigy Pharmaceutical Company, but not to the media, that they would not be filing a class-action suit. However, their tactics had worked. They received a lot of free air time and publicity, and many families who heard them believed them and began to fear such medication.

The Citizens Commission on Human Rights stated, in their flyer and during interviews, that: 1) Ritalin can lead to suicide, 2) Ritalin can be addictive, 3) Ritalin overdose can cause death, and 4) Ritalin is used in excess for too many children. None of these statements is correct.

A Model for Explaining ADHD and the Rational for Treatment

I explain ADHD and the role of medication to parents and the child using statements based on current research. I simplify some of the concepts to illustrate the issue.

I begin by saying that I would like to review "what the current research strongly suggests about ADHD." I explain that all of the facts are not yet in but that current research does give us some understanding. I then describe the hyperactivity, distractibility, and/or impulsivity, depending on which behaviors are present.

Hyperactivity. I explain that hyperactivity does not only refer to an individual who is running around and unable to be still. The term usually refers to one who is fidgety. At any time the fingers are moving, the pencil is tapping, the individual is up or down out of the seat. It seems that some part of the body is always in motion.

I then describe how the brain regulates muscle or motor activity. "There is an area in the brain that stimulates muscle activity. It is in the thinking part of the brain, the premotor cortex." I call this area the "accelerator." I proceed to describe another area in the lower part of the brain that decides how much of these messages will get through to the muscles, the ascending reticular activating system. I call this area the "brakes," and explain that normally there is a balance between the accelerator and the brakes for survival purposes and that the brakes appear to be the controlling factor. "If you are walking down the street at night and a dog jumps out barking, you cannot say to the accelerator, 'get me out of here.' Your brain just releases the brakes and you take off. Later, you will stop and recover by breathing hard and by rapid heartbeats."

Using this model, I explain that individuals with ADHD manifested by hyperactivity have a "brake" that is not working effectively. Thus, the accelerator is not as controlled and the individual has an increased amount of motor activity. Current research strongly suggests that the reason the brake is not working effectively is that there is a decrease in the chemical, called a neurotransmitter, needed to transmit messages from one nerve ending to another. The neurotransmitter that is suspected of being deficient is norepinephrine.

I then explain that the medications used to treat the hyperactivity work by increasing the amount of norepinephrine at the nerve interface in this lower part of the brain. Once the amount of this neurotransmitter reaches a normal level, the brakes can work effectively, controlling the accelerator. The result is a decrease in hyperactivity. I then reemphasize that these medications do not drug or sedate or tranquilize the individual. The medications make the individual "normal." To illustrate this, I use the analogy of diabetes; when people with diabetes are given insulin, they can function normally. Once the insulin is metabolized, the diabetic symptoms return. So, too, when the proper medication is used to treat ADHD, individuals can function normally. Once the medication is metabolized, the ADHD behaviors return.

Distractibility. I review the concept of distractibility, distinguishing it from the types of internal and external distractibility described in Chapter 3. I explain that in ADHD there is a specific type of distractibility that makes it difficult for these individuals to distinguish between relevant and nonrelevant stimuli in the environment. Thus, nonrelevant stimuli distract them and they have difficulty sustaining attention.

Another way of illustrating this concept is to explain that attention requires three steps:

1. Finding the appropriate stimulus and focusing on it.
2. Sustaining this focus.
3. When appropriate, releasing this focus so the person can move on to another stimulus.

Children and adolescents with ADHD appear to have difficulty with step 2, sustaining attention. Those who have difficulty with step 1 may have more of a psychological problem; they avoid the work or have difficulty getting themselves to start the work. It may be that individuals who have problems with step 3 show evidence of perseveration.

I go on to say, "the way the brain works is that when information comes into our brain through our eyes or ears, we run it through a 'filter system.' If it is important, it is allowed to pass through to the thinking part of the brain, the cortex. If it is not important, or if it can be handled at a lower level of the brain, it is monitored or processed at a lower level of the brain. That way, the cortex is not cluttered with every stimulus that enters the brain." This filter system appears to be in the same lower area of the brain as is the braking system. It is for this reason that two apparently unrelated behaviors—hyperactivity and distractibility—are often seen together.

To illustrate to parents how a normal "filter system" works, I give this example. "You might be in a store and many children are yelling 'mommy' or 'daddy'; yet, you only hear your child." Or, "if you are like me, you probably get in your car and drive home then suddenly realize that you were daydreaming and do not know how you did not get lost or hit someone. Somehow, your brain was able to monitor important information at a lower level, freeing your cortex to think of other things."

I explain that, like the braking system, the filter system is not working effectively because of a decrease in the neurotransmitter needed to send messages from one nerve ending to another within this system. The medication works by increasing the amount of this neurotransmitter, allowing the filter system to work normally. Once the filter system can work normally, individuals with ADHD can filter out unimportant stimuli. They are no longer distractible with a short attention span. They can now stay on task and block out unimportant sounds or sights in their environment like normal individuals.

Impulsivity. I start by explaining that we know less about impulsivity than we do about hyperactivity and distractibility. "Let me explain what we think might be the situation. When information is processed in the brain, it appears to arrive at a basic 'circuit board.' From there it is relayed to many areas of the brain for action and then comes back to this 'circuit board' for a reaction. It appears that this basic 'circuit board' is not working effectively. There may be some 'short circuits' causing the initial input to be responded to immediately, so individuals with ADHD do not stop to think before they talk or act. They are impulsive."

Using the same model described above, I explain that this basic circuit board appears to be in the same lower part of the brain as the brakes and the filter system, and that it is not working effectively because of a decrease in the amount of the neurotransmitter, norepinephrine. The medication increases the production of this neurotransmitter in this area of the brain, allowing the "circuit board" to work normally. Thus the individual is less impulsive and can stop to reflect before talking or acting.

This concept of a braking system, a filter system, and a circuit board is simplistic. However, by using it, parents, children, and adolescents can understand the problem and the rationale for treatment. Furthermore, I can work on the treatment plans by using these words to shortcut lengthy conversations. "The filter system is working better but not fully. He is still somewhat distractible. We should increase the amount of the medication."

The model also stresses the neurological basis for ADHD. It clarifies that the medication is specific and explains the reasons for using it. This model decreases the concerns of the parents that they are drugging their child to make the teacher happy or to make family life easier. The concept of making the child or adolescent "normal" and the analogy to diabetes is an important one for the parents and for children and adolescents with ADHD to understand.

Summary

A critical part of any multimodal treatment plan for individuals with ADHD is education. This educational process must include the individual with ADHD, parents, and family. Often this educational process is all that is needed to help the individual and family move ahead with the other parts of the treatment plan. If more is needed to proceed with the treatment, individual, parent, and/or family counseling or therapy may be indicated. These approaches are discussed in Chapter 9.

Chapter 9

Individual, Parent, and Family Counseling

The individual and family educational processes described in Chapter 8 often result in emotional and behavioral changes with everyone and an improvement in the behavior of children and adolescents with attention-deficit hyperactivity disorder (ADHD). The parents begin to be assertive advocates for their child, which results in more appropriate programs within the school system, and they begin to understand their child and change their parenting behaviors.

If, after these efforts, the clinician decides that either the parents, the child, or the whole family needs further help, specific counseling or therapy may be necessary. Behavior management techniques might be needed. A parent or both parents may need help with their emotional difficulties or in working through their resistance or struggles with the problems. The individual with ADHD may need help with his or her emotional or behavioral difficulties or with denial or noncompliance.

It might also be necessary for the parents to enter into couples therapy or for their child to enter into individual dynamic or behavioral therapy or for the family to start in family therapy. It is important to delay such decisions until this point in the process so the clinician can assess if the problems can be resolved with the educational process or the initial counseling efforts plus the use of appropriate medications. Also, by this time a better therapeutic alliance exists on which to build the next phases of clinical intervention.

Despite which form of clinical intervention is used, it is critical that the clinician consistently keep in mind the impact ADHD and the possible associated disorders can have on both the child or adolescent and on the family. It is equally important to understand how these disorders can impact on the treatment process.

Clinical Work With the Child or Adolescent

If, after the educational process, better school accommodations, and the use of appropriate medications, the student continues to have emotional or behavioral difficulties, individual therapy might be indicated. Individual, dynamic psychotherapy or cognitive-behavioral therapy might be considered. The techniques are the same as for other emotional or behavioral disorders.

The first phase of therapy continues to focus on education. The individual needs to understand the disabilities and the impact they have on every aspect of life. With this new knowledge, the individual can reassess the past and better understanding the difficulties experienced. This learning process often results in a more positive self-image and improved self-esteem.

Often, these individuals do not see their role in school, peer, and family problems. Therefore, the clinician should try to use recent events as examples for these individuals to understand their behaviors and to see what impact these behaviors have on others. Once they accept their role in what happens to them, they need to explore and learn alternative models of behavior as well as alternative coping strategies.

For children and adolescents with emotional problems manifested by a poor self-image, anxiety, and/or depression, the above approaches are helpful. For those with disruptive or antisocial behavioral problems, group or family therapy along with a behavior management system should be considered.

At every stage of therapy, it is important for the clinician to be aware of the impact that ADHD and any associated disorders can have on understanding, performance, or interactions in any setting. It is equally important that the clinician understand how these disorders can impact on the therapeutic setting and process.

Social Skill Training

Social skills needed for social competence include physical factors, such as good eye contact and posture; social responsivity, such as sharing; and interactional skills, such as initiating and maintaining conversation. Before starting in a social skill training program it is important to identify the individual's areas of social incompetence and the specific skills that appear to be missing.

There are many social skill training programs described in the literature. In general, they focus on a series of steps. The first step involves helping the child or adolescent develop a sensitivity for his or her social problems. This step is critical. Because of their impulsivity and inattention, some children with ADHD have only limited awareness of their socialization difficulties and may deny or project the source of their problems onto others.

The second step is having the individual generate alternative solutions for the identified problems. Here, the clinician and other group members can be of help. The third step involves helping the individual step-by-step through the process of learning the newly identified solution to the problem. Role-playing and practice are effective ways to learn these new behavioral solutions. The final step is to help the child or adolescent link the new knowledge to past events and difficulties as well as to future events. The individual is encouraged to try out the new social skills in new settings and to report back on successes and failures.

Clinical Work With Parents

The problems of children and adolescents with ADHD are not limited to the behaviors of hyperactivity, distractibility, and/or impulsivity. Thus even if medication controls these behaviors, other behaviors may need to be addressed, such as aggression, oppositional defiant behavior, conduct disturbances, academic difficulties, low self-esteem, depression, and poor peer relationships.

Work with the parents might focus on perceptions of the child or of themselves, based on past experiences with the child, that have not completely shifted with the educational process. A cognitive therapy approach might help with these difficulties.

A parent might have emotional or behavioral problems of his or her own or secondary to the stresses of raising a child with ADHD. Specific individual psychotherapy or the use of specific medications might be useful in these situations.

If there is marital stress, couples therapy might be indicated. This work might include forming a shared understanding of the child with ADHD and his or her needs and realizing how the previous lack of such understanding created stress between the parenting couple. The couple needs to work together to develop family strategies to handle the disruptive behaviors of their child and positive ways to help this child, as well as any other of their children.

Some parents need help being their child's advocate with the school system and with other activities. They need help finding the necessary information on ADHD, developing ways to work with the school, and finding parent support groups. They may need an advocate to work with them who knows the system and how to help the parents negotiate their way through it.

Clinical Work With the Family

Sometimes the family is under so much stress and is so dysfunctional that family therapy is needed before any educational or other therapeutic process can be considered. The early phases of this therapy might focus on giving the parents back the controls and on helping the child with ADHD feel safe not being in control. Specific behavior management approaches must be initiated. Later, when the family is functioning better, other clinical interventions can be considered as the needs are clarified.

Family therapy can be helpful in changing family members' perceptions and expectations of the individual with ADHD. Sibling conflicts can be addressed. The focus is often on changing unacceptable behaviors and on strengthening the positive relationships between family members. As siblings learn to understand and as they see positive changes in the family, they can become advocates for their sibling with ADHD at school, in the neighborhood, and in community activities. They can help with problems of peer behavior and peer rejection. A specific model for changing unacceptable behaviors in the family is discussed in Chapter 10.

Clinical Work With the School

It is hoped that the use of appropriate medication will lessen or stop the hyperactivity, distractibility, and/or impulsivity. It is important for the classroom teacher to understand how the medications work, what side effects might occur, how to observe behaviors, and how to communicate with the clinician managing the medication. If the use of medications is less than successful, the classmates and teachers will need to make special efforts to help the student in school.

If the student with ADHD also has an associated learning disability, it is hoped that the school will have identified this disability and that the appropriate special education interventions and classroom accommodations are in place. If the school has not identified the learning disability or started the necessary programs, parents need help to get the school to do so.

There is a considerable amount of new literature on the needs of the classroom and the roles of the teacher when working with a student who has ADHD. These guidelines often include the needs for those students who also have a learning disability. Such efforts focus on four areas: 1) establishing the best learning environment, 2) giving instructions and assignments, 3) modifying unacceptable behaviors, and 4) enhancing self-esteem.

The environment should be modified to address hyperactivity and/or distractibility. Students with ADHD should sit near the teacher's desk to increase the teacher's awareness and control. They should be seated in the front of the class with their backs to the rest of the class to minimize visual stimulation. These students should be surrounded with positive role models, preferably students who will not get pulled into inappropriate behavior. Distracting stimuli should be minimized, such as air conditioners, open windows or doors, and high-traffic areas. Transitions and changes should be handled with the awareness that these activities might be difficult. The student with ADHD might need increased structure and supervision in the hall, at lockers, at lunch, or on field trips.

When giving instructions or assignments, the teacher should maintain eye contact and make the information clear and concise. There should be a consistency with daily instructions and expectations. The teacher should be sure that students with ADHD understand the directions before beginning the task. If necessary, the teacher should repeat the instructions. Students with ADHD should be made to feel comfortable when seeking help. It is useful to require these students to write down all assignments each day. The teacher should sign the notebook to confirm that the assignments are correct and the parents should sign to show that the work was completed.

To modify behavior, the rules of the classroom should be clear and understood by the student. When rules are broken, the teacher should remain calm, state the infraction of the rule, and avoid debating or arguing with the student. It is helpful for the teacher to have preestablished responses or consequences for inappropriate behaviors. The consequences should be presented quickly and consistently. It is important that the teacher avoid ridicule and criticism.

Building or rebuilding self-esteem is important. The teacher should reward more than punish, and all good behavior and performances should be praised immediately. Ways should be found to encourage these students. If they have difficulty, it is important that the teacher find a way to reestablish contact and trust so that new solutions can be found and tried.

Summary

After the impact of individual and parent education and the use of appropriate medications are assessed, individual, parent, or family counseling or therapy may be necessary. The specific approach will depend on the assessed need. It is important that one clinician coordinate all efforts to be sure that each identified problem is addressed.

Whatever form of therapy (individual, couples, family, or other) is used, it is important that the clinician understand the impact of ADHD and any associated disorders on the problems being addressed.

Chapter 10

Behavioral Approaches to Treatment

The first phases of the multimodal approach to the treatment of attention-deficit hyperactivity disorder (ADHD)—parent and individual education and counseling along with the use of appropriate medication—usually help the family adapt and modify the family to better help the child with ADHD. If this child's behavior continues to be disruptive or dysfunctional to the family, it might be necessary to implement a more specific behavior management program. This chapter will discuss general concepts and approaches to changing behaviors as well as a specific behavior management plan.

By this time in the clinical process, children and adolescents have been informed about ADHD and what behaviors are a result of this disorder. It is important for them to understand what the medication can do to help and what it cannot do. For example, the appropriate medication can make an impulsive person less impulsive and more able to stop and think before talking and acting. However, these individuals now might need to learn how to think before acting and how to reflect so that they can learn from and use past experiences.

Parents, too, need to understand ADHD and why certain behaviors have existed. They need to know what the medications can and cannot do. If some of the problems exist after the medications are started they need to explore if this is because of the lack of medication (e.g., early morning before first dose or evening after afternoon dose wears off). They need to relearn parenting skills for this child.

It is easy to say that parents need to learn to be more tolerant of their child's motor activity level, yet it is not easy to live with someone who is always moving. Parents are told that homework should be done in a quiet setting with minimal external stimulation, but it is not easy to create such an environment in the average home. Clinicians often tell parents that they need to be consistent, provide structure, and try not to have changes in routines. However, it is not easy to do any of these suggestions in the typical, active, unpredictable world of the family. To complicate issues, one of the parents might have ADHD and be just as active, distractible, and/or impulsive as the child.

Thus, it is critical that the child be on the appropriate medication during all times when the ADHD behaviors interfere with functioning. Only in this way can the hyperactivity, distractibility, and/or impulsivity be controlled enough for normal family interactions and behavior.

If the child's behaviors are out of control or disruptive in other ways to the family, a specific behavior management approach is needed. To do this, behavioral observations must be made and the information learned must be developed into a specific program that fits the specific family and that is compatible with the philosophy of the parents.

Behavior Management Program

In an initial evaluation session with parents, a clinician might hear a child described as a tyrant who must have his way or all hell breaks loose with screaming, throwing things, hitting siblings, messing up his room, or "something." Later, the clinician finally meets this tyrant—a 4-foot, 70-lb little boy who could be picked up and carried under one arm. Where is the monster?

Then the clinician begins to work with the family and soon discovers that this child's behavior does dominate the family. The parents avoid many confrontations because they do not want to deal with the resultant behaviors. They look the other way until pushed so far that they have to react. By that time, feeling helpless, often the only possible reaction is anger; they yell, hit the child, or give out a punishment like "no television for one week" then have to back down because they have no way to enforce it or enforcing it leads to more confrontations and fights.

As the evaluation progresses, the clinician may gain clues or clarify the dynamics within the child or within the family that explain the behaviors. What is more likely to occur is that the clinician cannot clarify the underlying issues but can see that something must be done quickly; one has to "put out the fire" before an in-depth assessment can be considered. What is clear is that the child is in control and the parents are not in control or even are out of control. What may also be clear is that rather than supporting each other the parents are fighting with each other. This situation in the family causes anxiety in the child and is not compatible with healthy psychosocial development; it is dysfunctional for the parents and other members of the family as well.

Perhaps the clinician can see patterns. Without meaning to do so, the parents are reinforcing the very behaviors they do not want. The child acts badly and gets a lot of negative attention. The parents get upset and this proves to the child that she or he can control one part of the world, the family. This, along with getting what the child wants, is the reward for bad behavior. The other children become angry when they see the parents forced to surrender. Soon, the siblings may learn that the only way to get attention or to get what they want is to act badly.

Whatever the dynamics or initial cause, family dysfunction must be corrected. Parents must regain control. Children with ADHD must feel that they can be controlled. These changes are essential for the family. Such negative control of parents is unhealthy and unproductive. These children must learn more acceptable behavioral patterns in the family setting before the behaviors are used in the school setting, with peers, or in the community.

Once the behaviors are in control, the individuals with ADHD can begin to learn new and better techniques to function within the family and to cope with stress. Parents and children can rework styles of interacting and roles within the family. First the behavioral changes come, then awareness and insight develop.

It is not uncommon to find that children and adolescents who are out of control at home are functioning very well in school, at friends' houses, or when playing with friends away from the house. Sunday School teachers, activity leaders, and sports coaches might think these children are well behaved. Hence, one might assume that the behavioral difficulties are not neurologically driven or they would occur in every setting. If the behaviors are only expressed at home, it is possible that they reflect family dynamics or conflict. If the behaviors are only seen at home and medication is being used, a behavior management program might be needed just for the family. It is also possible that individuals hold in their frustration and anger all day so as to avoid trouble and then let it all out at home where it is safe to do so. Another possibility is that these children are on the appropriate medication and doing well during the hours the medication is working, during school. The addition of the medication for evenings and weekends might lead to a significant improvement in home behaviors.

The clinician might observe that the negative or aggressive behaviors are seen in school, with peers, during activities, and at home. In this situation, the possibility that the neurologically driven behaviors of hyperactivity, distractibility, and/or impulsivity should be seen as causing or contributing to the difficulties. Once medication is established, the behaviors might decrease or cease. If not, the behavior management program will have to include school and outside of the house activities as well as home time.

Behavior Management Concepts

Any behavioral plan must be based on several important concepts of learning theory. First, one is more likely to succeed in changing behavior by rewarding what is desired rather than by punishing what is undesired. Second, for a plan to work, the responses to acceptable and unacceptable behaviors must be consistent and must occur each time. Inconsistent responses or inconsistent response patterns may reinforce the negative behavior.

Parents must learn that there is no right or wrong way to raise children. They must collaborate in developing a plan that both find comfortable and agreeable. Once decided, they must act consistently and persistently.

Initially, they must be omnipotent. Their child will no longer be allowed to bargain, bribe, threaten, or try to provoke guilt. The parents make the rules; the parents enforce the rules; the parents' decisions are final. They must learn that if they "step into the arena" and agree to debate or argue with the child, they will lose. If a parent says it is time to go to sleep and a child says, "I want to stay up 15 more minutes," the answer must be, "I did not ask you what time you wanted to go to sleep. I said it is bedtime." Argue about the 15 minutes and it becomes 20 minutes, and then 30 minutes. Soon, the parents' frustration and anger will result in fighting. Later in the plan there can be flexibility, but not initially.

Developing the Initial Intervention Strategy

Initially, parents are usually overwhelmed. They have exhausted their choices of actions. They may feel helpless and like failures as parents. If there are two parents, there may be stress between them caused by disagreeing on how to handle their child's behaviors or blaming the other for the problems.

The clinician must be a firm and confident person. "I can help you. Work with me and we will get your child back under control. Then we can figure out how this happened and correct the more deeply rooted problems if there are any."

The first step is to ask the parents to collect data by observing their child's behaviors. Each is asked to collect data separately. They are told that the differences between the two will be very useful and are requested to record what really happens without worrying what the clinician will think. "We already know that things are not working well. Just record what you live so that we can begin to change things."

Parents will need a structure. The easiest model to use is an "ABC" chart. They record three things: the antecedent to the behavior (A), the behavior (B), and the consequences of the behavior (C). A typical entry might look like the example in Table 10–1.

Each parent will have a different list. One may be the firm disciplinarian and the other the easy-going, "give them another chance" type. Each parent will see and list different things. Each has different experiences and expectations. Father may come home at 6 or 6:30 P.M. looking forward to being with the children and playing with them. Frustrated and short of temper, mother may have had it by then and wants the kids to be quiet and to get their homework and other chores done so that they can go to bed.

Neither parent is right or wrong. The important goal is that both parents agree on their expectations and be consistent in requiring that they be met. Consistency is the key. Inconsistency reinforces the behavior; consistency stops the behavior.

Certain patterns should become clear for each column category and for overall behaviors. Certain antecedents lead to certain behaviors. The consequences that follow the same behaviors are inconsistent; one parent gets mad and yells at everything or other family members seem to get punished as much as the child who caused the problems. A common theme is that when children do not get what they want or are asked to do something they do not want to do, they misbehave.

Once the data are collected, they are analyzed. Patterns are looked for. The first task is to clearly define the unacceptable behaviors that need to be changed. Often, parents start with a long list of

Table 10–1. **Typical entry for an "ABC" chart**

Date/time	Antecedent	Behavior	Consequence
Monday 4:30 P.M.	Don't know; not there	John hit sister; she hit him back	Told both to go to room
6:00 P.M.	Talking to Mary	John teased her; she cried	Yelled at John
9:00 P.M.	Told John to get ready for bed	Refused to take bath, get in PJs; yelled at me when told	Took 30 minutes of reminding; finally hit him and he went to take bath

behaviors. Once the data are studied, the behaviors can be clustered into two or three major areas. By doing this, parents are not as overwhelmed and focus on a few major areas.

Frequently, the unacceptable behaviors fall into three basic groups: 1) physical abuse, including hitting sibling, hitting parent, hurting a pet, and damaging property; 2) verbal abuse, including yelling at sibling, yelling at parent, teasing, cursing or using other unacceptable words, and threatening someone; and 3) noncompliance, including not listening to what is said, not doing a requested chore, and defying a parent's request.

Once the behaviors are identified, it is useful for the clinician to study the relationship between the antecedents and the behaviors and to look for patterns. Are the behaviors more likely to occur if the child is tired, hungry, or about to be sick? Are the behaviors more likely to occur during the first hour after coming home from school? Are the behaviors more likely to occur when the child is off the medication? Do the behaviors appear to relate to the student's learning disabilities or sensory integrative disorder? Noting these patterns will be useful in helping the child or adolescent understand why he or she has difficulty and in helping the parents know when to be most alert to the possibility of problems.

Setting up the Initial Program

Once the parents have a clearer understanding of the behaviors that need to be changed, a plan can be developed. Each behavior should be defined as clearly as possible and an associated consequence, that can be imposed consistently, should be established. After the plan is worked out in great detail, the parents should introduce it to the family. The plan should include all of the siblings. Even if the siblings do not cause problems, it will not affect them negatively to be part of the program. By rewarding them for their good behavior, they will even benefit from it since it might have been that the "bad" child took so much attention that the "good" children were ignored or not thanked for being good. Furthermore, if a sibling is provoking or encouraging the negative behavior, it will become clear if he or she also is on the plan.

Parents need to understand the basic principles of behavior modification. Previously, they were punishing bad behavior and usually ignoring or occasionally rewarding good or positive behavior. By using this plan they will reward positive behaviors and withhold rewards for negative behaviors. Further, parents will have preplanned responses that they can use every time, preventing their child from catching them off guard and making them feel helpless and therefore angry. Each time a behavior occurs now, the response will be the same from both parents.

To better understand the importance of consistency, suppose a boy hits his sister five times in a week. On one occasion his mother was in such a rush she yelled at him but did nothing about the hit. On another occasion she was tired and did not want to deal with him so she pretended she did not see what happened. On the other three times she punished him. If this child gives up hitting his sister because mother tells him to, he has to give up hitting her 100% of the time. If he continues to hit her, he has a 40% chance of getting away with it. He would be a fool to give up the behavior. If a parent is consistent, the behavior will stop. If the parent is anything less than consistent, the behavior might persist or get worse. What follows is a three-step process to aid in creating parental consistency.

Step 1. Divide the day into parts. For example, on a typical school day there will be three parts: 1) from the time the child gets up until he or she leaves for school; 2) from the time the student returns from school until the end of the evening meal; and 3) from the end of this meal until bedtime.

Weekend or summer days can be divided into four parts by using meals as the dividers: 1) from the time the child wakes up until the end of breakfast; 2) from the end of breakfast to the end of lunch; 3) from the end of lunch to the end of dinner; and 4) from the end of dinner until bedtime.

Step 2. Make a list of the child's unacceptable behaviors. This list should be brief and limited to the major problems. If the three behaviors noted earlier are used, a list might read: 1) no physical abuse (define in detail; e.g., no hitting sister, pulling cat's tail, kicking mother, or breaking toys); 2) no verbal abuse (define in detail; e.g., no cursing, calling someone stupid, or teasing); 3) no noncompliance (define in detail; e.g., refusing to do what you are told to do). For younger children, the term "not listening" should be used. Make it clear that a parent will request several times. Then this parent will say, "If I have to ask you again, I will call it noncompliance." Any behavior continuing after this warning is called noncompliance. In this way the child or adolescent can never say, "But, you never told me I had to do this."

Step 3. The purpose of the plan is to reward positive behaviors. The child can earn one point for each behavior he *does not do* during a unit of time. Later, we will talk about "time out." With time out, too, the focus is on the positive and not the negative; thus, the wording is important. The parent says, "What you did is so unacceptable in this family that you must go to your room and think about the need to change what you do." The parent does not say, "Go to your room" with the connotation that doing so is punishment.

The child can earn points by not doing the unacceptable behaviors. One point is earned for each negative behavior not done. For example, suppose a boy gets up in the morning, does all of his chores, and gets to breakfast on time. He does not hit anyone but he does call his sister "stupid." As he leaves for school the parent would say, "I am pleased that you earned two points this morning. You followed all rules, and you did not hit anyone. I wish I could have given you the third point, but you did call your sister a name and that is verbal abuse." This parent might say to the sister, "I am happy that you earned all three of your points. Thank you for not calling your brother a name when he called you one." Remember, behavior is changed by rewarding what you want and not by punishing what you do not want.

A book or chart should be used to record the points. If the child is too young to understand points, stars can be pasted on a calendar or chart, or a jar can be filled with marbles to represent each point earned.

Each part of the day is handled in the same way. In the model designed above with three units of time during school days and four units of time on the weekend, the maximum number of points that can be earned on a school day is 9 and the maximum each weekend day is 12. The total for a week will be 69. These points can be used in three ways: a daily reward, a weekly reward, and a special reward. The points are counted daily and then continue to be counted weekly or accumulatively. The child should participate in developing the rewards. The parents make the final decisions but keep requests in mind. If the child says, "This is stupid. I won't participate," the parent should reply, "The plan starts tomorrow. Either you suggest what you would like to work toward or I will make the decisions for you."

Rewards must be individualized for each member of the family and each must be compatible with the family's style and philosophy. Rewards that involve interpersonal experiences are preferred to material rewards. The daily reward could be an additional half hour of television watched with a parent, being able to stay up 30 minutes later, reading a book or playing a game with a parent, or 30 minutes of special time with one parent.

The weekly reward might be going to a movie, out to eat with the family, having a friend sleep over, or any other special activity. Points are counted from Saturday morning to Friday night; thus the parents know if the child has enough points before the weekend starts. In this way, a baby-sitter can be lined up before any family activity. In the past, their child might have been impossible all week, yet would go out with the family on the weekend. Now, if not enough points are earned, this child will stay at home while the parents and other siblings go out.

A special reward might be something important that must be worked toward: a new bicycle, toy, or a special trip. It should take a month or more to accumulate enough points for this reward.

For the daily and weekly rewards, set a goal initially of 80% of the maximum number of points that can be earned. After a month of success (which might take several months to reach), the goal can be raised to 90%. It is preferable to never set the goal at 100%. No one can be perfect all the time. Any negative behavior early in the day or week could destroy all hope of a reward, and the child might give up.

For the plan described above, the child would need 7 points each weekday evening to get the reward (80% of 9 points). The child would need 55 points by Friday night for the weekend reward (80% of 69 points).

Time out. Before starting the plan, define which behaviors will be considered so unacceptable to the family that they will result in the child not earning a point plus being removed from the family for a limited time to think about the need to change this behavior. I always use this consequence for physical abuse. Other behaviors might be included. For the young child, 15 minutes is appropriate; for the older child or adolescent, 30 minutes is suitable.

Time out is to be spent quietly thinking about what happened and why the behavior needs to be changed. The child's room can be used if it is not equipped with a television, stereo, games, and other pleasurable distractions. If the child's room cannot be used, a guest room or laundry room might be suitable. The door is to be closed and the child is to be quiet. Each time the child opens the door or yells or throws something, the timer is reset to zero and the 15 or 30 minutes begins again. The child soon learns that unless he or she is quiet and cooperative, a 15 minute time out can last for hours.

Time out can be used away from home, as well. At a restaurant, the child can be taken to the car. If concerned about safety, a parent can stand near the car and watch. At a shopping center, the parent can find a safe place for the child to sit alone and can watch the child from afar for 15 (or 30) minutes.

In order for the plan to work, it must be specify expectations, behaviors that are rewarded, and consequences. Once initiated, the child will certainly find loopholes. Parents must promptly close each loophole.

A common example of where the child will find loopholes is time out. The child might be home with his mother. He is told to go to his room but he refuses to go. He child defies his mother, runs around the room, and dares her to chase him or runs out of the house. If this happens, the mother should not chase the child or drag him to his room. The plan is developed and explained in advance. The child knows that this plan will be implemented the minute he refuses to go to the assigned room for time out. This plan can have two parts:

1. The parents will announce a time that the child is expected to be in his or her room (e.g., 3 minutes from the time that the parent informs the child to go to the room). After that time, the child will need to spend 2 additional minutes in the room for every minute it takes to get to the room. This means that if the child does not go to the room until the father comes home 2 hours later, he or she will need to spend 4 additional hours in the room. This time cannot be counted after bedtime; thus it is spent in the room the next day, perhaps after school. Sometimes, the child will spend a weekend day making up the time out time because he or she tested the parent earlier. Soon, the child learns to listen.
2. The second part of the plan is for the child to understand that during the time he or she refuses to go to the assigned room the parent will say, "I will always love you dearly. However, when you abuse me as a parent, I do not choose to parent you." This means that the parent will not talk to the child nor interact in any way. When meal time comes, a place setting is set for everyone in the family but this child who may make his or her own meal and sit somewhere else. The child will miss meetings, sports practices, or games if the parent was supposed to drive. If the behavior persists till bedtime, the parent will not respond to the child nor put him or her to bed. Once the child begins the time out, parenting starts again.

Some parents find that this second approach too painful to consider. I remind these parent that allowing the unacceptable behaviors is more painful and potentially harmful to the child than the model suggested.

There are other frequent loopholes. For physical abuse, the child does not earn a point and goes to a quiet room to think; thus the events are stopped. What about verbal abuse? For the first event, the child will not earn a point. What does the parent do for the remainder of the time in this time period if this child is verbally abusive again? I suggest that for the second occurrence, the child must go to the quiet room for 15 to 30 minutes to think about the fact that such behavior is not acceptable in the family and he or she must change. What to do for noncompliance once the child does not earn a point is harder to handle. What do parents do when the toys still need to be put away or a bath is still needed? Later in this chapter, several alternative plans are described.

This reward-point system along with a time out system will work. The key is to be consistent. Parents must be encouraged to develop the plan and to implement it. The child will test them; but, if they stick to it, the child's behaviors will improve. To some parents' surprise, once the external controls work and the child functions better, he or she is happier rather than more frustrated. Even with visible improvement, the plan must be continued. If stopped too soon, the behaviors will return.

Setting up the Second Phase of the Plan

The first phase of intervention provided external controls. The goal of the second phase is to help the child internalize the controls. Now the effort shifts to building these controls into the behavioral patterns of this child. The first phase continues; however, a more interactive rather than omnipotent approach is used by the parents.

Once the unacceptable behaviors are under better control, *reflective talking* can be introduced. Initially, these discussions are held after the fact. The best time might be at night while sitting on the bed. For example, a child has been in a fight or a yelling match. He has spent time in the quiet room. Later in the day a parent sits with him in private and discusses what happened. "Fred, I am sorry you had so much trouble this afternoon. I love you, and I do not like being angry with your behavior or having to ask you to remove yourself from the family. What do you think we can do to stop such things from happening?" Let him talk. At first he may only make angry accusations of unfairness or of others causing the trouble. To that the parent might respond, "I don't know if your brother was teasing you before you hit him or not. I was not there. But, let's suppose that he did. What else could you have done? By hitting him you got into trouble and he did not. There must be a better way. Maybe you could have told me what you thought he was doing." Such conversations may have to occur many times before the child begins to think about his or her behavior and to consider alternative solutions to problems. It is important that the parent not only point out the behavior, but also offer alternative solutions.

Gradually, the parents can point out themes. "You know, Mary, I notice that you are most likely to get into trouble right after you come home from school. Do you suppose that you hold in all of your problems all day so that you will not get into trouble and then let it out the first time you are upset at home? If so, maybe we can do something to help. Maybe, as soon as you come home you and I can sit in the kitchen, have a snack, and talk. Maybe if you tell me about your day and the problems you will feel better and will not have to act out your feelings."

Soon the parents will be able to present reflective thinking before the fact. "John, you and I both have learned that if you keep playing with your brother once the teasing starts, there will be a fight. Do you remember what we talked about? What else could you do?" Or, "Alice, you are forcing me to be a policeperson and to yell at you or punish you. I do not like doing that. I'd rather enjoy being with you than yelling at you or punishing you. Why do you think you force me to be a policeperson? Remember what we talked about the other night? Do you want to try some of the ideas we talked about?" Gradually, the child or adolescent will begin to try the new behaviors.

The child can learn from hearing the parents openly discuss feelings and thoughts. Parents can let the child understand how they feel—angry, sad, afraid, or worried. They can role model how to handle these feelings. "I am so angry with what you did that I cannot talk to you. I am going into the other room to calm down. Later, we can talk." Not only will this parent feel more in control, but will have demonstrated a way to handle angry feelings.

It is important that parents begin to explain or role model acceptable ways for their child to handle feelings. Many parents are quick to tell their children how they may not show anger, sadness, or disappointment, but they do not teach them acceptable ways of showing these feelings. Anger is a normal feeling and children must learn how to handle these feelings in an acceptable way. Can they yell as long as they do not curse? Can they stamp their feet or slam the door shut as long as they do not break anything? Watch out for confusing messages. One parent in the family yells or throws things when angry. The other parent pouts or goes to a room alone when angry. But, when the child gets angry and starts to yell he or she is told, "You may not do that." If the child walks off pouting, the parent says, "You come back here. I am talking to you." It is acceptable for families to have different rules for the adults and the children. However, parents must then teach their children acceptable ways for them to express feelings in the family.

Additional Models

In addition to the basic plan, other concepts can be added to address specific problems. These plans may work best around issues of noncompliance. What do parents do after the child or adolescent has not earned a point, yet the requested behavior is still required? The basic concepts are the same: the parents are in control, the rules and consequences are consistent and persistent.

Handling Chores

To avoid any confusion about chores or other duties expected by the family, parents must make a detailed list of their expectations. Individual chores might include putting dirty clothes in the hamper, making one's bed, and picking things up off of the floor. Family chores might include setting the table, loading or emptying the dishwasher, and vacuuming. Place the list where it will be seen. Clarify if these chores are to be rewarded by money or if they are expected as part of family responsibility. If the family chores are to be shared on different days, make a clear list of what each child is to do each day.

If the chores are not done, what will be the consistent consequence? Several models are presented here. Each gives the controls back to the parents, but the choice is left to the child. If the child completes the chore, there is the expected reward. If a task is not done, there is a clear consequence.

The "maid service." Establish that all parent services are not supplied free of charge. If chores are not done by a set time, a parent will do them, but for a price. Make a list of the chores and set a reasonable fee for each one. (Be realistic for the age and financial resources of the child.) For example, the charges may be 25 cents to make the bed, 50 cents for picking up things from the floor of their room, and 50 cents for putting the bike in the garage. Then, the parents must stop arguing, reminding, or nagging the child. If the chore is done by the preset time, fine. If it is not done, then the parent completes it without commenting. At the end of each day or week, the parent submits a bill for the service. If the child receives an allowance, the parent might present a bill at the end of the week. For example:

Allowance:	$5.00
Maid service:	3.75
Balance due:	$1.25

The child might get upset and ask how lunch drinks or snacks are to be bought. Parent should reply, "Think about that next week when you decide not to do a chore." If the child does not get an allowance, use birthday or savings money. If there is no such money or if the child owes the parent more than the allowance, that child should be given specific work details to earn the money owed. "I will pay you $2 an hour to clean the garage. You owe me $3; so, I expect you to work 1 hour this weekend."

There will be no more getting angry, no more reminding, and no more fights. The child has only two choices now—to do the chores and get the rewards or not do the chores and pay someone else to do them.

The "Sunday box." Set up a "box" in a secure place: a closet or room that can be locked or the trunk of a car. Make it clear that any items left where they should not be after a predetermined time of the day (e.g., toys, bike, books, coat, and shoes) will be placed in this box. It will not be emptied until Sunday morning. This means that if a favorite game or bike or piece of sports equipment is not put away, it is lost until Sunday. If the objects are clothes or shoes and cannot be done without, the child must pay a fee to retrieve them early.

This plan has worked so well in some families that a wife placed her husband on the plan as well. His clothes and other belongings that had not been put away disappeared into the Sunday box.

Handling Property Damage

When a child damages property during an outburst, the initial response will be based on the plan in place. If this behavior is considered physical abuse, the child will not earn a point and must spend time in a quiet room thinking. If a larger consequence to the behavior is deemed necessary, the child could be forced to pay to repair or to replace the item. The money could come out of an allowance, or if the amount is large, the funds may come out in installments until the debt is paid off. If this model is not possible and the child does not have a savings account, a way for the child to earn the money should be created. Assign other than expected tasks and pay by the hour— cutting the grass, washing clothes, washing the kitchen floor, or cleaning the garage are good examples. By using this model, the first time a child gets angry and kicks over and breaks a lamp, the child will learn that at $2 per hour, it will take 25 hours to replace a $50 lamp. Now this child may begin to think before acting. And this is the goal, to get the child to think about the consequences of the behavior before acting.

Handling Dawdling

Parents often reinforce dawdling by reminding, nagging, yelling, screaming, and then, in anger, doing the task with or for the child. All this behavior does is teach the child that it is possible to get away with the behavior, force the parents to help, and get the parents upset. Instead, define the limits for a behavior then establish clear consequences.

For example, a child may not get dressed on time. He or she is not openly oppositional, but is so busy playing or looking out of the window that tasks just are not completed. The time to meet for the school bus gets closer and the child has not yet dressed or eaten because he or she is dawdling and playing. The parent goes into the bedroom, yells at the child, and quickly dresses him or her so that there will be time to eat and catch the bus. The child has succeeded in getting the parent upset and angry and in getting the parent to help. Before stating the consequence of the behavior, it is important in this situation to establish whether or not the difficulty getting dressed might relate to a learning disability (e.g., sequence, organization, or motor), a sensory integrative disorder, or ADHD behaviors present because the child is not on medication during these hours.

For this type of behavior, the parent might first establish the rules. For example, the parent might say, "The kitchen is open until 7:30 A.M. You must be dressed to enter. If you come in before 7:15, mother or father will make you a hot breakfast. If you come in after 7:15, you may have cold cereal. No food is served after 7:30. You will have to go to school hungry." The child is expected to be ready to leave for the bus by 7:40 A.M.

What should the parent do if at 7:40 A.M. the child is still not dressed? Older children and adolescents should be told that if they miss the bus or car pool, they can walk or take public transportation to school. The parent should not write a note if the child is late or absent; thus the school might issue a detention. The child must deal with the consequences: "Sorry the problem is yours. Maybe tomorrow you will get dressed." A child who remains at home must stay in his or her bedroom during normal school hours. There should be no television or interactions with parents.

If the child is young and the school cooperative, another plan can be developed with the help of the bus driver, the classroom teacher, and the principal. The child should be told of the plan in advance: when it is time to leave for the bus, quietly take all of the clothes that have not yet been put on and place them in a bag. Wrap the child in a robe or coat and walk him or her to the bus, pajamas and all. The bus driver, having been briefed, smiles and says hello. The child gets on the bus with the bag of clothes, and the parent then calls the principal to have the teacher alerted. If the child dresses on the bus, fine. If he or she arrives at school in pajamas, the teacher quietly asks, "Would you like to go to the bathroom and get dressed?" The child will not starve without breakfast on this day but will have learned that dawdling no longer works. Only he or she is affected by the behavior.

This approach might work in other situations. At bedtime, whether in pajamas or still in street clothes, put the child in bed and turn out the lights. When the family is ready to leave for a movie or a visit or a shopping trip and the child is not ready by the requested time, the parents should leave with the rest of the family. If the child cannot be left alone, have a sitter on call for the early phase of this approach so that the parents can follow through with the plan. Once the sitter is called, it is too late to change plans, even if the child dresses quickly. After a time or two when the child or adolescent loses rather than the parents or the rest of the family, this individual will get the message: finish your tasks on time or accept the consequences. You lose, not the rest of us.

Summary

When a consistent behavioral plan is used in a family, unacceptable behaviors begin to change to more acceptable behaviors. Parents regain control and confidence in their ability to parent. Children and adolescents learn that they can be controlled, and that they will not be overwhelmed by not being in control. They are usually happier. Now all of the positive experiences with the family reinforce the behaviors as well.

If the plan does not work or does not work as well as desired because of learning disabilities, a sensory integrative disorder, or other associated disorders or because the ADHD behaviors are not being managed by medication during all critical hours, these clinical issues must be addressed. The behavioral program should clarify these problems and help to focus on the needs.

If the plan does not work either because one parent (or both) does not follow the plan or defeats the plan or because the child cannot give up being in control or the need to be punished due to intrapsychic conflicts, more intensive individual, couples, or family therapy might be needed.

Chapter 11

Treatment With Medication

The use of medication to treat what is now called attention-deficit hyperactivity disorder (ADHD) was first described in 1937. During that year there was an epidemic of viral encephalitis. Some children, as they recovered from this disease, were observed to be hyperactive and distractible. Dr. C. Bradley, a pediatrician, prescribed a stimulant medication (Benzedrine) for these patients and found that they became less active and distractible. Stimulants have been used to treat these behaviors ever since. It is important for parents to understand that medications have been used to treat ADHD for more than 50 years. Follow-up studies into adulthood show these medications to be effective and safe with no apparent long-term side effects. Between 70 and 80% of children and adolescents with ADHD treated with the appropriate medication show improvement.

Stimulant medication will decrease or stop the hyperactivity, distractibility, and/or impulsivity. These medications do not treat learning disabilities if they are present. For some individuals with ADHD manifested by hyperactivity, medication can result in improved motor control and possibly in improved handwriting. Individuals who are distractible might be better able to organize their thoughts when speaking or writing because of a decrease in interference with the thinking process. Short-term memory might improve because of a better ability to stay on task and concentrate. Individuals with impulsivity might perform better because they can now reflect before answering a question. For the same reason, they might be better able to use cognitive strategies for learning. However, the basic underlying psychological processes associated with the learning disabilities appear not to be changed.

Initially, the stimulants were thought to produce a paradoxical effect. Stimulants calmed these individuals. Sedatives were found to stimulate some of them. As described in Chapter 6, the current research suggests a different mechanism of action. ADHD is presumed to be caused by a neurotransmitter deficiency. The stimulants work by increasing the production of this neurotransmitter in the brain, probably norepinephrine in the ascending reticular activating system.

ADHD might be found among children or adolescents who have

mental retardation or other disorders such as fragile X syndrome, pervasive developmental disorder, or closed-head trauma. The use of stimulant medications is appropriate in these clinical situations, as well. Stimulant-induced seizures in individuals with a seizure disorder appear to be unlikely but must be considered before medication is started.

There is no established protocol for treating ADHD with medication, although I will present an approach I find helpful. The protocol discussed should be seen as one possible model for thinking through each step of the clinical treatment process. Each clinician must individualize the model for the patient being treated. My discussion of each medication, its effects, and side effects should not be seen as a substitute for the clinician reviewing the drug manufacturer's and professional literature for each medication before using it.

Clinical Premises

It is important that the necessary differential diagnostic process be considered before establishing the diagnosis of ADHD. If the clinician establishes this diagnosis, it is presumed that the behaviors are neurologically based. Therefore, because ADHD is not a school disability but a life disability, the need for medication must be assessed for each hour of each day. As stated often in this book, to place children and adolescents on medication only during school hours on school days will result in them doing better in school. However, they may continue to have difficulties within the family and in interactions with peers. To take these individuals off of medication that is successfully treating ADHD and then send them to day camp or sleep-away camp over the summer is to invite problems. The concept of "drug holidays" started with the concern that the use of stimulant medications might inhibit growth hormone and thus growth; therefore, it was believed these individuals needed to be off medication so that they could grow. This concern started after one study suggested such a possibility. Several major studies done since then have showed that growth hormone is released at night, when the child is off medication. More details on this issue will be presented later in this chapter. Although the final answer is not available, the general view is that the clinician does not have to worry about growth problems.

Once the appropriate medication is found, several important points must be determined: 1) the amount of medication needed per dose, 2) the dose frequency, and 3) when the individual should be on medication. An approach to answering these questions will be discussed for medications currently in use.

As discussed previously, there is nothing magical about puberty for these children. The only way to determine if children and adolescents continue to need medication is to take them off of the medication once or twice a year and to observe if the ADHD behaviors return. If they do, medication should be restarted. If they do not, the medications can be stopped.

A Clinical Protocol

I find it helpful to have a format to follow when treating individuals with ADHD. In the absence of an established protocol, I will discuss the one I use as a possible treatment approach.

Treatment begins using one of the medications in what I call *group I*. If these medications do not help or if the side effects create a problem that cannot be clinically resolved, *group II* medications are tried. If these medications do not help or only help control some of the behaviors, a combination of group I and group II medications may be tried. If the patient still does not respond or if side effects require the clinician to try something else, *group III* medications are then considered (Table 11–1).

Group I medications. These are stimulant medications and are proposed to work by increasing the concentration of catecholamines (dopamine and/or norepinephrine) at the synaptic cleft. They include methylphenidate (Ritalin), dextroamphetamine (Dexedrine), and pemoline (Cylert).

Group II medications. Two tricyclic antidepressant medications (TCAs) are used. They are proposed to work by inhibiting the uptake of catecholamines, primarily norepinephrine, thus, increasing

Table 11–1. **Medications for the treatment of attention-deficit hyperactivity disorder**

Group I medications
  Methylphenidate (Ritalin)
  Dextroamphetamine (Dexedrine)
  Pemoline (Cylert)
Group II medications
  Imipramine (Tofranil)
  Desipramine (Norpramin)
  Clonidine (Catapres)
  Bupropion (Wellbutrin)
Group III medications
  Thioridazine (Mellaril)
  Carbamazepine (Tegretol)
  Lithium

the concentration of this transmitter at the synaptic cleft. They are imipramine (Tofranil) and desipramine (Norpramin); desipramine is a metabolite of imipramine.

TCAs may decrease the hyperactivity and distractibility. For reasons that are not clear, they might not be as helpful in decreasing the impulsivity. Therefore, if a TCA helps with some of the behaviors and not with the impulsivity, one of the group I medications might be used in conjunction with it.

Clonidine (Catapres) is not a TCA; however, it may be considered with the group II medications because it appears to reduce the endogenous release of norepinephrine by activity at the autoinhibitory presynaptic receptors, and thus it decreases norepinephrine. Yet, as discussed later, it may help reduce the behaviors of ADHD.

Bupropion (Wellbutrin) has been considered as a medication for ADHD. Early studies showed that it may be effective. Although it is not a TCA, it does block the reuptake of dopamine.

Group III medications. About 70–80% of children and adolescents with ADHD will respond to one of the medications in group I or group II or to a combination of these medications. However, 20–30% will be "nonresponders." Research to date does not clarify why some individuals do not respond to the medications. It is possible that the diagnosis is incorrect. Another possibility is that these individuals have another form of an attentional disorder. Another concept being considered is that in these individuals, the presumed neurological problems are not in or are only in the reticular activating system. To use the symbolic model discussed in the previous chapter, perhaps the hyperactivity is not due to a poorly functioning "brake," but due to increased activity by the "accelerator" in the cortex. Possibly, distractibility is not caused by a poorly functioning "filter system," but due to an oversensitive cortex. And, possibly, the impulsivity is not due to a poorly functioning "circuit board" but due to "short circuits" in the cortical areas. That is, perhaps the difficulties are not in the lower brain but in the cortical areas. Medications in group III are presumed to "calm" the cortex; they include thioridazine (Mellaril) and carbamazepine (Tegretol).

There is another small subgroup of nonresponders that now might begin to be clarified. There have been several case reports of young adults who were diagnosed as having ADHD as children and who responded well to the use of stimulant medication for years, but they each developed a full bipolar disorder in their early twenties. In these cases, there was a family history of unipolar or bipolar illness. Also, the childhood descriptions included possible mood swings or changes in behavior. Because the precursor behaviors in childhood for bipolar illness are not known, one must consider the possibility that ADHD and bipolar disorders share a common neurochemical theme or that for some the behaviors of ADHD might be the earliest clinical evidence of this disorder. Such children and adolescents may respond very well to the use of lithium.

Some children or adolescents present with a complicated clinical picture suggesting multiple areas of brain dysfunction. They might show behaviors characteristic of individuals with pervasive developmental disorder. In addition, they might have learning disabilities and/or ADHD. These individuals might show some improvement with the group I or group II medications. When group III medications are tried, some improvements may be found as well. It is possible that for this group both the cortex and the reticular activating system might be involved. Using this clinical lead, the use of a group I or a group II medication along with a group III medication will provide the best results. It is presumed that medication is needed for both brain sites.

I sometimes try to explain to parents why there are different medications by using the analogy of a lake that does not have enough water in it. There are two ways to increase the level of water in the lake. One would be to pour more water into the lake, the other to build a dam that blocked the outflow of water from the lake. The group I medications (stimulants) appear to work by increasing the amount of water in the lake, that is, by increasing the production of the neurotransmitter. The group II medications (TCAs) work by blocking the outflow of the water, that is, by slowing down the breakdown process of the neurotransmitter.

Group I Medications: The Stimulants

As noted, three stimulant medications are used in the United States: methylphenidate, dextroamphetamine, and pemoline. Methylphenidate is structurally related to amphetamine. It acts by releasing stored dopamine from reserpine-sensitive presynaptic vesicles, decreasing dopamine reuptake, and inhibiting monoamine oxidase activity, as well as possibly by direct postsynaptic agonist activity. The sum effect is an increase in dopamine and norepinephrine at the synaptic cleft. Dextroamphetamine increases dopamine and norepinephrine neurotransmission by stimulating the release of newly synthesized dopamine at the synaptic cleft, by inhibiting presynaptic reuptake of these transmitters, and by inhibiting monoamine oxidase activity. The sum effect is also an increase in dopamine and norepinephrine at the synaptic cleft. Pemoline is structurally dissimilar to amphetamine. It has minimal or no sympathomimetic activity and primarily influences dopamine neurotransmission.

It is difficult to predict to which stimulant medication an individual with ADHD will respond best. Some will respond poorly to one and have a positive response to another. Neurological soft signs, electroencephalograms, and neurochemical measures do not appear to be useful predictors of stimulant responsiveness. The clinician must judge which one to try first.

Each of these medications has shared and unique characteristics, effects, and side effects. The discussion in this chapter covers many of these issues; however, the clinician should review the pharmaceutical and professional literature before recommending or prescribing any medication.

Methylphenidate and dextroamphetamine are available in both short-acting and long-acting forms. Pemoline is only available in a long-acting form.

Methylphenidate is available in 5-, 10-, and 20-mg tablets and in a long-acting Ritalin-SR 20 tablet. Ritalin-SR 20 contains 20 mg of methylphenidate and releases approximately 10 mg initially and 10 mg 4 hours later. Although there are references to the amount needed per kilogram of body weight, the amount needed by each individual does not seem to relate to body weight. A young child and an adult might need the same amount. The average dose is 15–30 mg/day in divided doses. Some individuals may require more. The Food and Drug Administration (FDA) guidelines recommend up to 60 mg/day; however, more may be used if clinically necessary and carefully monitored. If the medication is metabolized rapidly and only lasts about 3 hours, it might be necessary to give four or five doses per day; thus using more that 60 mg daily in some cases.

Dextroamphetamine is available in 5-mg tablets and in long-acting spansules of 5-, 10-, and 15-mg strength. As with methylphenidate, the dose is established more by clinical observations than by the specific body weight. The FDA guidelines set the lower age limit at 3 years old. The upper dose limit recommended is 40 mg/day; however, more can be used if clinically necessary.

Pemoline is available in 18.75-, 37.5-, and 75-mg tablets and in 37.5-mg chewable tablets. It is administered as a single oral dose each morning, although an evening dose may be used. The recommended starting dose is 37.5 mg/day. The dose can be increased gradually by 18.75 mg each time. The maximum recommended daily dose is 112.5 mg, although older adolescents and adults may need a higher dose.

Because methylphenidate is the most frequently used of the

group I medications, it will be used here as a prototype to discuss the clinical use of these medications.

Methylphenidate (and dextroamphetamine) in the short-acting form begins to work in 30–45 minutes in most individuals. Recent studies have shown that it is not necessary to take the medication on an empty stomach. Food does not impair absorption of these medications; thus it can be given with a meal or after a meal. Each dose lasts between 3 and 5 hours. It appears that the amount needed per dose is a reflection of the speed with which the medication is absorbed and metabolized. The functional blood level may be the same for the individual who needs 5, 10, 15, or 20 mg per dose.

There is some clinical evidence suggesting that the effect of stimulant medication in preschoolers is more variable than with older children and adolescents. Therefore, these medications should be used along with parent education and counseling, behavior management efforts, and a review of appropriate preschool placement.

Given these clinical factors, the three points noted at the beginning of this chapter have to be addressed: 1) how much medication is needed per dose, 2) how often the medication is needed, and 3) during what time periods the medication should be used.

The initial medical workup should include measurements of height, weight, pulse, and blood pressure. ADHD individuals should be observed for tics and involuntary movements, and a history of tic disorders in the family should be obtained. If pemoline is to be used, liver function tests should be performed. No such tests are required for methylphenidate and dextroamphetamine. Medical follow-up at each visit should include observing for tics and involuntary movements and measuring pulse, blood pressure, weight, and height. If pemoline is used, liver function tests should be done every 4–6 months.

Establishing the Dose

Dose-response relationships vary widely among individuals. Although the therapeutic dose range is believed to be 0.3–0.7 mg/kg per dose for methylphenidate and 0.15–0.5 mg/kg per dose for dextroamphetamine, the best way to establish the dose needed is not by obtaining frequent blood levels but by the clinical monitoring of therapeutic effects and side effects.

The usual starting dose is 5 mg each time taken. For a younger child, 2.5 mg may be considered. The dose can be increased by 2.5 or 5 mg per dose every 2–3 days until the maximum benefit is noted. I usually start each individual on a three-times-a-day, 7-days-a-week program. Only in this way can the parents, the individual, the teachers, and I assess the benefits from the medication. Later, the specific times of coverage can be determined.

Clinical judgment is used to establish the best dose. I start at the lowest dose I believe might possibly work and increase the dose by 2.5 or 5 mg until maximum benefit is reported by all. At times, I might increase the dosage in steps to build in a model for observation. That is, I might increase the morning dose but not the noon dose (e.g., 10 mg at 8 A.M. and 5 mg at noon and 4 P.M.). I then ask the teacher to observe if the student is better able to sit and attend in the morning as compared to the afternoon and evening.

Feedback from the teachers and parents is critical in assessing the improvement in the hyperactivity, distractibility, and/or impulsivity. One efficient way to do this is to ask a parent to talk to the teacher each day at the end of the school day and then relay this information to you. Thus one call can provide feedback from the school and home.

When determining the best dose to achieve maximum benefit, it is useful to increase the dose until this point is reached. As will be detailed later, there are two side effects that suggest that the dose is too high. If either occurs, the dose should be lowered. One side effect is emotional lability: the child or adolescent becomes upset easier than would be normal for this individual, crying or having tantrums. The other side effect is that some children or adolescents appear to be "in a cloud" or "in a daze," possibly described as glassy-eyed.

I find it best to start with a short-acting form of the medication until the appropriate dose and time of dose is established. Then, a longer-acting form may be considered because if a child is started on Ritalin-SR 20 first, the clinician cannot judge if the individual might have needed less per dose. If 10 mg per dose is too high for this person, the use of the long-acting form might result in emotional lability or spacey behavior. Once the dose is established, the long-acting form can be considered if the amount needed for two consecutive doses equals the amount released in the long-acting form.

Establishing the Dose Interval

The average length of action for a short-acting tablet is 4 hours. However, for some individuals, the medication may last 2.5–3 hours and for others it might last up to 5 hours or more. Thus, the dose interval must be established for each individual. There is nothing special about using methylphenidate every 4 hours.

The dose interval is determined clinically, using the feedback from the parents, the individual, and the teacher. As an example, a child is placed on 5 mg of methylphenidate at 8 A.M., noon, and 4 P.M. daily. If the feedback throughout the day is good, that dose interval may be best. If the teacher says, "You know, John is great in the morning. But, about 11 or 11:30 A.M. he begins to wiggle in his seat and cannot stay on task. He is perfect again after he gets his noon medication," perhaps, the dose interval for John is 3 hours. He may need his medication at 8 A.M., 11 A.M., and 2 P.M..

If the teacher reports, "Alice is great in the morning. Only, between 12:30 and 1 P.M. she gets so upset. If I look at her the wrong way, she cries (or, she seems to be in a cloud and cannot be reached). By 1 or 1:30 P.M. she is fine again." Perhaps, for her the dose interval is 5 hours. The noon dose starts to work at about 12:30 to 12:45 P.M. For a short period of time, she is getting too much medication. The interval dose for her might be every 5 hours. She may take medication at 8 A.M., 1 P.M., and 6 P.M.

Sometimes parents will report that their child or adolescent is significantly improved when on the medication. The morning dose is given just before the child leaves for school at about 7:45 to 8 A.M. However, between the time the child gets up and the time the medication starts to work, he or she is impossible. The hyperactivity, distractibility, and/or impulsivity result in difficulty staying on task (getting dressed on time) and in sibling problems (nagging, yelling, and fighting). In this situation, it would be ideal to provide the benefits of the medication during the early morning hours, as well. The first dose may need to be given earlier and the following doses adjusted accordingly. For example, the parents might need to wake the child 30–45 minutes before he or she has to get out of bed to take the first dose. By the time the child gets up, the medication is working. The morning goes well for all. If this time is 6:30 A.M., the child may need to take the later doses at 10:30 A.M. and 2:30 P.M. A fourth dose may be needed at 6:30 P.M.

The same reasoning can be used for other problem situations. Suppose the child gets the first dose at 8 A.M. right before leaving for school and gets into trouble on the school bus. But by the time school starts, the child is fine. The morning dose may have to be given earlier so that it is working by the time the child gets on the bus. Or, if the third dose is at 4 P.M. and wears off by 8 P.M. and if the parents report behavioral difficulties from 8 P.M. until bedtime at 9:30 or 10 P.M. (e.g., the child has trouble getting ready for bed, following routines, and getting along with siblings), it might be appropriate to consider a fourth dose at 8 P.M.

The theme is that the medication lasts about 4 hours. The clinician, the parents, and the individual with ADHD need to learn just how long the medication lasts and then review units of time to assess if the ADHD behaviors are interfering with functioning. If the behaviors are interfering with functioning, medication coverage for these hours may be indicated. Medication time models need to be individualized for each individual.

Establishing the Periods of Time to Be Covered

Because ADHD is a neurologically based disorder, children and adolescents with this disorder will be hyperactive, distractible, and/or impulsive throughout their awake hours. It is important to clinically assess each individual in his or her total environment to determine during which hours medication coverage is needed. There are no confirmed contraindications to the use of these medications on a continuous basis. Furthermore, clinical research has shown that the amount of the medication in the blood at any one time is the same for individuals who take the medication on a chronic basis as it is for the individual who takes a single dose. Thus, medication can be programed around 3-, 4- , or 5-hour units of time without concern that time is needed to accumulate the appropriate blood level or that such treatment will make the child or adolescent worse.

The key to determining when the individuals should be on medication is to observe the effect of the ADHD behaviors. Hyperactivity, distractibility, and/or impulsivity can be a problem whenever such behaviors interfere with what is expected. Each behavior may interfere with functioning in the classroom and can interfere likewise with any school-like activity such as religious education, Sunday School, or homework. They can also interfere with scout meetings or related activities. Some individuals (or their coaches) note that they can concentrate and play sports better on the medication.

The impact of some of these behaviors will depend on the age, grade, school demand, and family style. For example, a first or second grader might have little or no homework. Therefore, if this child is distractible, medication will be needed during school hours but may not be needed after school hours if this child spends most of this time playing outside and the family doesn't mind the fidgetiness. However, the same child might need medication for these hours when older and homework demands increase.

Weekends and holidays must be thought through in the same way. If the behaviors of ADHD interfere with expected activities or performance, medication will be needed. As an example, suppose the child is an 8-year-old boy who is hyperactive, and the family plans a weekend trip. They will drive for 4 hours to get to his grandparents' house. Once there, he will run around and play with his cousins for most of the time. Finally, there will be the 4-hour ride home. He might need medication coverage during each 4-hour car ride and during the quiet family dinners. However, he might not need medication during the remainder of the weekend.

To determine which hours must be covered by medication, I try to educate the parents and the individual on how the medication works. If they know that it starts to work in about 30–45 minutes and that it lasts 3–5 hours, and if they know that on the medication there is a decrease in the difficult behaviors, they can think through units of time with the clinician and decide when medication is needed. Often the individual with ADHD will be the best clinician. One recently asked me if he could use the mediation when he played soccer. He told me, "I can concentrate on the game so much better when I am on the medicine."

Using Long-acting Medications

Once the dose, time of dose, and time of coverage is determined, the clinician can consider using a long-acting form of the medication. For methylphenidate, the long-acting form can be considered only if 10 mg is needed for each of two successive doses. Recent studies have suggested that for some individuals the Ritalin-SR 20 appears to take longer to be effective and only lasts 4–5 hours. Thus it may not work as well as taking two individual 10-mg doses 4 hours apart. If the Ritalin-SR 20 tablet is chewed instead of swallowed whole, the blood level is unpredictable and the individual might show evidence of too high a dose part of the time and too low a dose other times. For dex-troamphetamine, the options for a long-acting form are greater because there are 5-, 10-, and 15-mg spansules available, each lasting about 8 hours.

Pemoline only comes in a long-acting form. The dose taken each morning must be determined. Because the medication must be used each day to maintain the proper level, the time of coverage is not an issue.

Side Effects and Their Management

To review the side effects most often seen and how they may be managed, I will use methylphenidate as a prototype of a group I medication. Later, I will note the less frequent side effects listed in the pharmaceutical literature.

The two most frequently found side effects are loss of appetite and difficulty falling asleep at night. Also, but much less frequently, some individuals will complain of a stomachache or headache. Of even less frequent occurrence, tics may occur. As noted earlier, there are two side effects that suggest that the dose of the medication may be too high for the individual: emotional lability and a confused, cloudy cognitive state.

Loss of appetite. Methylphenidate may decrease an individual's appetite. This side effect may decrease over the first several weeks and cease to be a problem. If it persists, it needs to be addressed. The first step is to observe eating patterns. The medication may take the edge off of the appetite; thus, the child might not finish meals but may eat candy, cake, and other sweets. If this is the case, parents need to limit such sweets unless the meal is eaten. Some children are not hungry and do not eat their lunch at school. They return home at about 3:30 P.M. when the noon dose is wearing and are hungry. They eat a huge snack and then cannot eat dinner. Parents need to offer smaller or lower-calorie snacks after school.

For some, the aforementioned approaches do not work and the child continues to eat less than before starting the medication. He or she may lose weight or not gain weight. The next step is to try to create "windows of opportunity." I try to give the first dose after breakfast. Since medication is not given in the middle of the night, the child should have a normal appetite in the morning. I accept that lunch will not be great. The parents might try to make a meal that the child is more likely to want (e.g., a jelly sandwich rather than a tuna fish sandwich). Teachers should be alerted that the student may not eat lunch and that this is alright. For some children, this free time might mean the need for more supervision. Rather than giving the third dose at 4 P.M., I try to hold off until dinner time (5:30 to 6 P.M.). In this way, there can be a period of "time off" from the medication so the appetite can return. The child might need more structure and supervision during this time, and homework might be delayed until later. If none of these approaches works, a group II medication might have to be considered.

Sleep difficulties. Some children and adolescents have difficulty going to sleep when they take methylphenidate. This problem often decreases or goes away over the first 2–3 weeks. If it does not, an intervention is needed. For some, it is the medication that keeps them awake. For others, it is the lack of medication that keeps them awake. Each possibility must be explored. Each reason leads to a different management approach.

When it is the medication that makes falling asleep difficult, and if the problem occurs only occasionally, diphenhydramine (Benadryl) may help. A dose of 25–50 mg at bedtime might be helpful. It is important for these individuals to know that this medication is not a sleeping pill. Therefore, they cannot read or play until they get sleepy. However, if they lie quietly in the dark and try to sleep, the medication may help them fall asleep. This medication might help the child or adolescent return to a pattern of sleeping and then be phased out. For some, it might be needed occasionally. It is best not to use it on a regular basis. If the sleep problems persist, the 4 P.M. dose may have to be decreased or stopped. If this change creates behavioral problems in the afternoon and evening or when doing homework, a group II medication might have to be considered.

A lack of medication might cause sleep problems with some. If the individual takes the medication three times a day, he or she is functioning "normally" from about 8 A.M. to about 8 P.M. That is, he or she is no longer hyperactive, distractible, and/or impulsive. The medication wears off and the behaviors return, sometimes in greater intensity. He or she is not use to being this way and cannot lie still, block out stimuli, and fall asleep. For these individuals, a fourth dose of medication at about 8 P.M., allowing for the decrease or stopping of the ADHD behaviors may allow them to fall asleep with no difficulty.

I know of no way to distinguish which of the above reasons causes the sleep problem. I inform parents and their children of the possibilities and ask them to help decide which is causing the problem. I ask that they pick an evening when staying up very late will not cause a problem, maybe on a Friday or Saturday. I have the individual take a fourth dose of the medication at 8 P.M. If the medication is causing the sleep problem, they will have great difficulty going to sleep. I advise these families that if this happens, diphenhydramine can be used. If the added evening dose of the medication results in the individual going to sleep with no difficulty, I have learned that it is the lack of medication that is causing the problem. This fourth dose might be used everyday.

Stomachache. The reason for this side effect is not known. It is my suspicion that the cause relates to the fact that the stimulant medications are sympathomimetic; thus they decrease gastrointestinal motility, which results in food remaining in the stomach longer. However, I have prescribed a high-fiber diet based on this possibility with no success. I know of no approach that corrects this side effect. If it persists, a group II medication may be needed.

Headache. The reason for this side effect is not known. If the headaches persist, it will be necessary to try a group II medication.

Tics. Tics might begin immediately or months after the medication is started. The most common tics are of the head or neck muscles. Some will involve the pharyngeal muscles, resulting in sniffing, snorting, or coughing. Once the tics begin, it is preferable to stop the medication and change to a group II medication. Sometimes, it takes up to 6 months for the tics to completely stop.

As noted earlier in this chapter, if there is a family history of a motor tic disorder or of Tourette's disorder, there is an increased concern that the stimulant medication might initiate this disorder earlier than it might have been genetically set to start and that discontinuing the medication will not result in the tics going away. If such a tic disorder already exists, there is the concern that the stimulant medication might aggravate the disorder. Thus it is important to ask if there is a family history of a tic disorder before starting a group I medication and to make a notation of the answer in the medical records.

Clinical research data suggest that if there is a history of a motor tic disorder or Tourette's disorder or if such a disorder has been diagnosed, ADHD should not be treated with a stimulant medication. The use of a neuroleptic, such as haloperidol (Haldol), clonidine, or desipramine should be considered. However, some professionals recommend that with such a history or diagnosis, the group I medications can be used. If tics develop, they should be treated. Each clinician must decide what to do. My preference is to use a group II medication or other medication if there is any concern about a tic disorder.

Emotional lability and cloudy cognitive ability. As noted earlier, these two behaviors suggest that the dose of the medication is too high for the individual and should be lowered. The reason for these behaviors is not known. These side effects stop once the dose is at the appropriate level.

Height growth impairment. It is not clear if stimulant medications impact on growth. If they do, dextroamphetamine may retard growth more than methylphenidate. If present, the slowing of height gain rarely reaches clinical significance and is generally related to dose and duration of treatment. A return to projected height is reported if sufficient time is allowed after treatment. It may be that if medication is continued into the time of epiphyseal closing (ages 15–18), growth recovery may not occur. It is important to understand that studies show that height loss, if it occurs, may be only 1–3 cm. Overall, data suggest that stimulant usage contributes less than 3% of the variance in adult height outcome and produces no significant decrement in eventual height for most children. The effect, if any, is not due to a change in the level of growth hormone (which is released primarily at night) but may be due to an alteration in cartilage metabolism.

My clinical understanding of the data leads me to use the medication without concern about height. I do not feel there is a need for vacations off medication nor to stop the use of these medications before age 15. Clinicians must be aware of the literature and establish their own views on this issue.

Other side effects. The pharmaceutical literature describes other cardiovascular, central nervous system, gastrointestinal, allergic, and endocrine difficulties. These side effects are uncommon. However, the clinician should be familiar with these possibilities before starting group I medications.

Unlike the other stimulant medications, pemoline can impact on liver function. Thus, as noted earlier, periodic liver function tests should be done.

Other Clinical Issues

Preschool children. When stimulant medications are used with preschool children, there may be a higher frequency of side effects, especially emotional lability, manifested by sadness or irritability. It is possible that these side effects are secondary to the preschool child's sensitivity to the medication and to the need for lower doses.

Tolerance. No research data have shown the appearance of a tolerance to stimulant medications over time, except possibly with Ritalin-SR 20.

Rebound. Some children and adolescents seem to experience a rebound effect when the methylphenidate is metabolized and the blood level drops. They not only return to their previous level of hyperactivity, distractibility, and/or impulsivity, but may be excitable, talkative, impulsive, or have insomnia. This rebound behavior might last for an hour or more. Often, the problem lessens or stops after several weeks on the medication. If the rebound does not stop, the last dose of the day might need to be decreased. If this change creates a problem, one might try to add a fourth dose to see if the evening can be handled without the rebound and the child can go to sleep before the dose wears off. If nothing works, a change to a group II medication might be needed.

Impact of other medications. The pharmaceutical literature covers this topic in great detail. I will discuss the more common medications only. For some individuals, the additional use of a decongestant medication might increase the hyperactivity or make the individual feel agitated. The use of theophylline might do the same. In each case, if the newly introduced medication needs to be continued over a long period of time, a change to a group II medication might be considered. If the new medication is to be used for a short period of time, the amount of methylphenidate might be increased for this period of time.

Some sedatives and antihistamines appear to decrease the effectiveness of the methylphenidate. The individual appears to have "broken away" from the medication, and the ADHD behaviors return. It may be necessary to increase the dose of the methylphenidate while these other medications are used, returning to the appropriate dose after they are stopped. A problem might occur when a child on methylphenidate gets a cold and is placed on an antihistamine. The child becomes more hyperactive, distractible, and/or impulsive. Physicians may conclude that the child is older and may need more medication. With an increase in dose, the behaviors improve. However, once the cold improves and the antihistamine is stopped, the child might become emotionally labile or appear to be in a cloud. Not knowing why this happened, the physician might stop all medication to "reassess," and the child begins to have problems at school and home.

Another situation might occur before surgery. The child or adolescent is given a preanesthetic, usually a short-acting barbiturate. Rather than calming down and getting sleepy, this child may become more active. More barbiturate may be given and the child gets even more active.

Fever. For reasons that are not yet understood, when children with ADHD have a fever they often become calm and relaxed. The ADHD behaviors decrease or stop. Some parents report that they love it when their child has a fever because he or she will cuddle in their lap and be calm. It is unclear at this time if a child on methylphenidate should go off of the medication during the period of the fever. I usually do so and find that the behaviors remain under control.

Other Information

In the earlier literature, some professionals raised the question of "state-dependent" learning (i.e., will children retain what they have learned while on a medication once they stop taking it?). Studies indicate that there are no "state-dependent" problems with methylphenidate or with the other group I medications. Because the dose appears not to be related to weight, children and adolescents on a group I medication usually do not need a higher dose as they grow in size or height. Many may need the same dose for years.

At one time the use of a group I medication with a child or adolescent with a seizure disorder was considered unwise. However, clinical studies have shown that having a seizure disorder need not be a contraindication to using stimulant medications. Children and adolescents with a seizure disorder should be evaluated on an individual basis; however, the use of a group I medication can be considered.

The question of addiction and abuse is noted in the pharmaceutical literature. At the low doses used, addiction has not been reported to be a problem. Current studies suggest that dextroamphetamine probably carries a higher risk of addiction than methylphenidate and pemoline probably carries relatively less risk. For those children or adolescents with ADHD who also have a conduct disorder, special supervision may be needed to observe if the medications are being sold to peers. There is no evidence that substance abuse is increased by the use of stimulant medications. Families should be informed of the concerns but assured that under proper management, addiction is not likely to occur.

Group II Medications: TCAs

Group II medications are used if the group I medications do not work or if they produce side effects that cannot be clinically managed. Another reason for their use might be an attempt to obtain a smoother, more even effect from medication when a group I medication does not last long enough or when there is a rebound effect. Both imipramine and desipramine are long acting; thus the time for each dose and the time period covered by the medication are not issues.

Imipramine

This medication is available in 10-, 25-, and 50-mg tablets. The FDA guidelines suggest use from age 6 years and older. There is no apparent relationship between plasma level and clinical improvement. A starting dose for children might be 10 mg in the morning and 10 mg at bedtime. Unlike the group I medications, imipramine might take 3–5 days before its benefits can be assessed. The dose can be increased every 3–5 days until the maximum benefit is reached. Usually, the additional dose can be added in the evening or in the morning. If the feedback suggests that the child or adolescent is not doing as well during the middle of the day, the total dose can be divided into three parts and taken in the morning, early afternoon (thus avoiding the need to give it at school), and evening. A maximum dose of 2.5 mg/kg a day (1.12 mg/lb a day) is recommended.

Imipramine works best in decreasing hyperactivity and distractibility. My clinical experience has shown it to have less of an effect on impulsivity. If the impulsivity persists, a small amount of a group I medication might be added. Often, because the group I and group II medications each produce a relative increase in the suspected neurotransmitter at the synaptic cleft, less is needed of each when used together. If a group I medication was stopped because of side effects, the lower dose needed in conjunction with a group II medication may not result in the side effect.

Side effects. Imipramine may produce electroencephalographic changes at doses higher than the recommended level. It should not be used if the individual has a seizure disorder because it might lower the threshold for seizures. It cannot be used if the individual is on a monoamine oxidase inhibitor (MAOI). Adolescents must be warned that imipramine may enhance the nervous system depressant effects of alcohol.

The primary clinical side effect is sedation. If the individual complains of being tired or is observed falling asleep in class, the dose may have to be lowered, given in divided doses during the course of the day, or given primarily at bedtime. Other clinical side effects might include a dry mouth or constipation. Although very uncommon, imipramine can impact on blood cell production, primarily causing a pathological neutrophil depression, and can impact on liver function. Thus, a differential blood count and a liver function battery should be done initially and every 4–6 months thereafter while the medication is being used. If changes are noted, the medication should be discontinued.

TCAs can cause heart blockage or arrhythmias. There might be a prolongation of the PR interval, widening of the QRS complex, inversion or flattening of T-waves, tachycardia, and ventricular arrhythmias. These effects appear to be dose related and uncommon in children and adolescents. Most deaths associated with these drugs have been with adults and have occurred after deliberate or accidental overdose or in patients with preexisting abnormalities in cardiac conduction. To detect a preexisting cardiac conduction defect, a baseline electrocardiogram (ECG) is recommended. Follow-up ECGs should be part of follow-up care.

Desipramine

Desipramine is a metabolite of imipramine. It is available in 10-, 25-, 50-, 75-, 100-, and 150-mg tablets. At this time, the pharmaceutical literature does not recommend its use for children. It is not listed as a treatment for ADHD. However, studies show that it can be effective for ADHD. The recommended starting dose is 10–25 mg (0.5–1.0 mg/kg) daily and then increased weekly by 1.0 mg/kg per day. The maximum recommended dose is 5 mg/kg per day.

The contraindications and the side effects are the same as for imipramine. Three cases have been reported of a child dying suddenly while being treated with desipramine. With one 8-year-old boy, there had been no known cardiac abnormalities. He had been on the medication for 2 years as a treatment for ADHD. Plasma levels of desipramine obtained from all three of these children were in the therapeutic or subtherapeutic range. Although there was no clear link, the studies suggested possible cardiac toxicity. The details available on these children are outlined in the case examples below.

Case 1

In March 1987, an 8-year-old boy collapsed at school and experienced cardiac arrest during transportation to the hospital. The child arrived in the emergency room with ventricular fibrillation. He was converted to normal sinus rhythm but subsequently had cardiac arrest and died.

He had been on Norpramin, 50 mg/day, for approximately 6 months for the treatment of ADHD. The desipramine plasma level obtained 1 hour after cardiac arrest was 85 ng/ml. The autopsy, which was restricted to the family, was considered nondiagnostic.

According to the coroner's report, the child had undergone a muscle biopsy procedure 4 years before his death. During the procedure, the child developed paroxysmal atrial tachycardia. The biopsy report concluded that the child had an "undefined skeletal muscle disorder." The coroner's report also noted a family history of sudden cardiac death.

Case 2

The case cited in the Norpramin package insert involved an 8-year-old boy who had no prior known cardiac abnormalities. In October 1987, he collapsed on the floor at his home. Paramedics were called and cardiopulmonary resuscitation was administered. The child was asystolic at his arrival at the hospital. He was resuscitated and transferred to a children's hospital where he arrived with a rapid ventricular rhythm. The child's condition deteriorated and he died.

This child had been treated for approximately 2 years with Norpramin for "hyperactive behavior disorder." The dose administered is unknown. A letter from the medical examiner who handled this case noted the cause of death as cerebral hypoxia due to apparent cardiac arrhythmia. The toxicology blood level of desipramine was 10 ng/ml. It is not know if this blood specimen was obtained before or after death.

Case 3

The description of this case is based entirely on newspaper accounts (*Pittsburgh Post-Gazette*, June 15 and 16, 1988; *Pittsburgh Press*, June 16, 1988). According to these reports, a 9-year-old boy was being treated with Norpramin for depression for approximately a year after a motor vehicle accident in which he suffered a broken leg and a concussion. Shortly after running five laps around the gymnasium at school, he complained of nausea and collapsed.

He was taken to a local hospital and transferred to a children's hospital where he died 3 days later of "pneumonia, an irregular heart-beat and swelling of the brain." The toxicology blood level of desipramine obtained antemortem (an unknown amount of time after the arrest) was 120 ng/ml. The sequence of these events was not further clarified. The treating pediatrician at the hospital stated that tests obtained 2 months before death indicated no cardiac problems. The boy's mother had died of congestive heart failure 3 days after giving birth to him.

The currently available information about these sudden deaths is limited but suggests that the children were not receiving unusually high doses of desipramine nor were their blood levels reported to be above the therapeutic range at the time they were obtained. In each case, the cardiac status of these children before the event is not known. Thus there is no way to show that desipramine caused a direct toxic effect that led to sudden death in healthy children.

It could also be possible that the deaths occurred in children with preexisting but undetected cardiac conduction defects or structural anomalies and that the deaths were completely unrelated to exposure to desipramine. Another suggestion is that desipramine exacerbated a preexisting, undetected cardiac conduction defect or structural anomaly. Finally, desipramine could have had unusual effects on an immature cardiac conduction system. There are no data to support any of these possibilities.

The current literature suggests increased caution in the use of desipramine and, possibly, other tricyclic drugs in the treatment of prepubertal children. Although the limited information available does not provide an adequate basis for developing an informed recommendation, it is suggested that an ECG with a rhythm strip be obtained at baseline and during medication "loading" and steady state with specific emphasis on measurement of the Q-T interval (QT). It may be contraindicated to administer tricyclic antidepressants to children who have prolonged QTs at baseline; and, it may not be wise to continue the medication in any patient whose QT exceeds 0.425–0.450 seconds while on medication. A more comprehensive cardiac assessment may be indicated in children with a positive family history of cardiac conduction defects or sudden death.

Clonidine

If the use of a group I medication results in minimal improvement or in side effects that cannot be controlled, the use of clonidine might be considered. Its mechanism of action was discussed earlier.

Clonidine appears to be more helpful in treating hyperactivity and aggressiveness. There may not be as significant of an improvement in distractibility. This medication appears to improve frustration tolerance and compliance with children and adolescents who also have an oppositional defiant or conduct disorder.

Clonidine comes in 0.1-, 0.2-, and 0.3-mg tablets and in a transdermal therapeutic system (TTS patch). The patch comes in different strengths programmed to deliver either 0.1, 0.2, or 0.3 mg of clonidine per day for 1 week. The usual dose is 0.15–0.3 mg/day. The average dose for a child is 0.025–0.3/per day and for an adolescent 0.3–0.4 mg/day. The medication is given in divided doses three to four times a day, at mealtimes and bedtime.

The usual starting dose is one-fourth to one-half of the 0.1-mg tablet (0.024–0.05 mg) given in the evening. The dose can be increased by adding a similar dose in the morning. If needed, a third similar dose might be added in the morning. Clonidine is a short-acting medication; thus, such frequent doses may be necessary. Once the best dose is established with oral medications, the use of the patch might be considered. It might take several months to observe benefits from the medication. The patch provides slow absorption through the skin and avoids the marked changes in blood levels when using the tablets. It is suggested that one-fourth to one-half of a Catapres-TTS patch be used.

Side effects. The most frequent side effect is sedation, usually seen during the day. This sleepiness is most likely to occur during the first 2–4 weeks and then often decreases. Clonidine, as an antihypertensive agent, may produce hypotension. In children, a 10% decrease in systolic pressure may be detected, but this change generally produces no clinical symptoms or discomfort. The patch might produce an allergic skin reaction and have to be discontinued.

The initial medical workup should include a recording of blood pressure and pulse. Blood pressure and pulse should be obtained weekly during the first month of clonidine treatment. Once the dose is stabilized, these measurements can be obtained every 2 months. Information on sedation should be obtained on a regular basis.

If clonidine appears to work but some behaviors remain, and the clinician is hesitant to increase the dose, methylphenidate or dextroamphetamine may be added. The two in combination might produce better results.

Bupropion

As mentioned earlier, bupropion hydrochloride (Wellbutrin) has been suggested for use when all other group I and group II medications are ineffective. The research on the use of this medication has not yet been published. The clinician is referred to the pharmaceutical literature for suggested dose and possible side effects.

Group III Medications

Each of the medications in group III is very different and must be discussed separately. Often the amount of medication needed is less than would be used for the primary clinical disorders usually treated by these medications. Because each is different, it is necessary for the clinician to review the pharmaceutical literature in detail and not to rely on the brief information provided here.

Thioridazine

Thioridazine (Mellaril) comes in 10-, 15-, 25-, 50-, 100-, 150-, and 200-mg tablets as well as in a concentrate form of 30- or 100-mg strength and in a 25- and 100-mg suspension. The FDA approves the use of this medication for ADHD starting at age 2 years. The starting dose can be as low as 10 mg in the morning and 10 mg at bedtime. The effect of the medication might not be noticed for 3–5 days. The dose can be increased by 10 mg each 3–5 days until maximum benefit is noted. The recommended maximum dose is 30 mg/kg per day (approximately 14 mg/lb). If the child or adolescent does not do as well during midday, the dosage can be given in three divided amounts during the course of the day.

The main side effect noted is sedation. If sedation occurs, the dose may have to be decreased, given in divided doses, or given primarily at bedtime. At the low doses used for ADHD, extrapyramidal symptoms as seen in tardive dyskinesia are not common; however, the clinician must look for them. Dryness of mouth or nasal stuffiness might be seen.

Akathisia or motor restlessness is sometimes difficult to distinguish from certain forms of hyperactivity in children and can be confused with a worsening of symptoms or agitation. This clinical condition is characterized by pacing, restless feelings in the legs, a central state of agitation, dysphoria or irritability, and an inability to sit still. It is uncommon with children. Parkinsonian symptoms such as muscular rigidity, finger and hand tremor, drooling, akinesia, and masklike faces are rare in preschool-aged children but may occur in school-aged children and adolescents.

Other very infrequent side effects are hypotension, agranulocytosis, cardiovascular effects, acute dystonic reactions, seizures, and pigmentary retinopathy. Photosensitivity may occur and sun screens should be used routinely to prevent severe sunburns until sensitivity to sun is determined.

There are no specific laboratory tests needed before the use of this medication. During follow-up visits no specific studies are needed. Careful observations for the presence of abnormal movements should be documented. The following case example illustrates the type of child who benefits from the use of a group III medication.

Case 4

John was adopted at age 3 from an orphanage in Central America. At the time of adoption he was significantly underweight and did not walk. Once with his American family he gained weight and showed significant growth in motor and language skills. He was described as very active from the time he began to walk. He started preschool at age 4 where he was described as very active and highly distractible. At home he was described as "wound up," unable to control himself, unable to pay attention, and always on the move. John played poorly with peers and often got into fights.

Based on a comprehensive evaluation he was diagnosed as having learning and language disabilities as well as ADHD. In addition to family counseling and a behavior modification plan, he was started on medication. Over a 6-month period he was tried on methylphenidate, dextroamphetamine, imipramine, imipramine plus methylphenidate, and clonidine. These did not decrease his hyperactivity, distractibility, or impulsivity. He was finally tried on Mellaril. The dose was slowly increased to 25 mg tid. At that point he showed improvement with a decrease in his hyperactivity, an increase in attention span, and some improvement in his impulsivity. As of this writing, he remains on the Mellaril.

It was suspected that his learning and language disabilities plus the behaviors of ADHD reflect a pervasive neurological dysfunction. John's case reflects the probable impact of malnutrition plus possible other stresses during his early life and possibly during pregnancy.

Carbamazepine

Carbamazepine (Tegretol) is available in 100- and 200-mg tablets. A starting dose of 100 mg at bedtime is recommended. For children under age 12, the dose can be increased by 100 mg given in the morning and at bedtime for a recommended maximum dose of 1,000 mg. For individuals over age 12, a maximum dose of 1,200 mg can be considered. The dose needed for ADHD is usually less than that needed for control of a seizure disorder.

It is important to monitor the blood level to maintain a therapeutic level and to avoid a toxic one. The more common side effects are dizziness, drowsiness, nausea, and vomiting. Because of possible side effects impacting on the hemopoietic or cardiovascular system or on liver function, careful monitoring is needed. More details on side effects can be found in the pharmaceutical literature.

Lithium

Lithium carbonate comes in 300-mg capsules and 300-mg tablets as well as in 450-mg controlled release tablets. The amount needed will vary with each individual.

Side effects might include hand tremor, polyuria, and mild thirst. Transient and mild nausea and general discomfort may be seen. These side effects may decrease over time. More details on side effects can be found in the pharmaceutical literature. The following case example illustrates the successful use of lithium.

Case 5

Allan was first evaluated at age 10. He had a chronic and pervasive history of hyperactivity, distractibility, and impulsivity.

During the 2 years before my consultation, he had been on several group I and group II medications with no to minimal benefit. When he was taking methylphenidate, 20 mg every 3 hours (five times a day), he was less hyperactive.

Allan lived with his father and stepmother. A detailed history revealed that his biological mother had been in a psychiatric hospital on two occasions. The father remembered that she was depressed and her mother also struggled with depression. Upon further questioning, Allan was described as moody and as having mood swings from very agitated to very quiet. He was started on lithium. Over a month he reached a dose of 1,200 mg/day and the serum level reached a therapeutic range. His behaviors improved and he became calmer, more attentive in school, and less impulsive. Individual and family therapy was started to help him and his family work on the residual behavioral problems.

Summary

Medication to treat ADHD must be seen as part of a multimodal approach that includes education, counseling, and behavior management along with the medication. If any of the associated disorders are present, they must be treated, as well.

This chapter is meant to be a guide for consideration when treating children and adolescents with ADHD. It should not be seen as a substitute for reading the pharmaceutical and professional literature.

Chapter 12

Other Nonmedication Treatments

Two areas of clinical observation suggest possible themes relating to attention-deficit hyperactivity disorder (ADHD). One observation is that there is a relationship between nutrition and behavior. No clear patterns or interventions have been clarified, yet the relationship is apparent. The other observation is that there is a relationship between allergies and behavior. It is hoped that future research will add to the understanding of these relationships and behavior, especially the relationship food and allergies may have with ADHD. These observations have lead to proposed treatments. None have been successful; however, efforts in these areas continue. For now, what is known or proposed will be reviewed.

Nutrition and Behavior

The first major effort to relate a nutritional issue to ADHD was proposed by Dr. Benjamin Feingold, a pediatric allergist. His concepts and the research on this theory and therapy are discussed first. Other professionals have proposed other nutritional concepts. These are reviewed later.

Food Additives and Preservatives

In *Why Your Child is Hyperactive* (Random House, 1985), Dr. Feingold proposed that synthetic flavors and colors in the diet were related to hyperactivity. He reported that the elimination of all foods containing artificial colors and flavors as well as salicylates and certain other additives would stop the hyperactivity. Neither in this book nor in any of his other publications did he present research data to confirm his theory or the success of the treatment. All findings were based on his clinical experience. He and his book received wide publicity. It was left to others to document whether he was correct or incorrect. Several research centers were funded by the federal government to begin to do research in this area. Basically, two different types of clinical studies were done—dietary-crossover designs and specific-challenge designs.

Dietary-crossover studies. In these studies, hyperactive children were randomly assigned either to the elimination diet or to a control diet and then crossed over to the other treatment. The researchers found ambiguous results. Improvement in behavior was noted in a few children but only by the teachers when the control diet was given first and followed by the elimination diet. The findings were not noted when the order was reversed. In another study, the parents noted improvement with the elimination diet; however, the objective measures of hyperactivity showed no improvement. These studies suggested that there may be a subset of hyperactive children, particularly younger children, who respond to some aspect of the elimination diet, but either such a group is extremely small or the effectiveness of the diet is much less dramatic and predictable than had been described in previous anecdotal reports.

Specific-challenge studies. The dietary-crossover studies showed that a different research approach was needed. The strategy was changed from testing the general efficacy of the overall elimination diet to considering the specific involvement of the artificial colors or flavors with the hyperactivity. In this specific-challenge design, the children were maintained on Feingold's elimination diet throughout the study. Periodically, the children were given (challenged with) foods that contained the suspected offending chemical (e.g., artificial food colors). Measures were taken to note if the hyperactive state was precipitated or aggravated by this challenge.

The data from these studies suggest that there does appear to be a subset of children with behavioral disturbances who respond to some aspects of the Feingold diet. However, as noted above, the controlled clinical studies indicate that this group is small. Furthermore, with notable exceptions, the specific elimination of synthetic food colors from the diet did not appear to be a major factor in the reported responses of a majority of these children.

Research conclusions. In 1982 the National Institutes of Health held a consensus development conference on defined diets and childhood hyperactivity. This conference was sponsored by the National Institute of Child Health and Human Development. A panel of experts reviewed all of the existing research and listened to reports and testimony from people who wanted to present to the group. They reached conclusions similar to those presented above.

Specifically, they reported that "these studies did indicate a limited positive association between the 'defined diets' [i.e., Dr. Feingold's diet] and a decrease in hyperactivity." The panel noted that there was insufficient evidence available to permit identification beforehand of this small group of individuals who may respond and to determine under what circumstances they may derive benefits. The panel members noted that the defined diets should not be used universally in the treatment of childhood hyperactivity at this time.

Two later literature reviews reached the same conclusions. The Feingold diet is not effective in treating hyperactivity in most children. There may be a small percentage, 1–2%, who appear to respond positively to the diet for reasons that are not yet clear. There is no way for the clinician to identify in advance which individuals might be part of this small group.

In clinical practice one observes a small percentage of children with ADHD who become more active when they take medications with red or yellow dyes (e.g., penicillin) or when they eat large amount of foods with these dyes (e.g., cereals and drinks). It is possible that these are the children who might benefit from the elimination diet.

A few recent studies provided data supporting the therapeutic success of the Feingold Diet. The final answers are not in; however, the preponderance of studies support the views of the consensus conference.

Refined Sugars

Clinical observations and parent reports suggest that refined sugars might promote adverse behavioral reactions in children. Two theories have been proposed for this possible reaction. One is that certain sugars (e.g., glucose) could influence brain neurotransmitter levels and thus the activity level in hyperactive children. Another possibility is that carbohydrate intake influences the level of essential fatty acids. These fatty acids are essential for the synthesis of prostaglandin in the brain. Insulin is required in this critical step to activate the prostaglandin precursors. Thus the level of essential fatty acids could be influenced by carbohydrate intake and could secondarily influence insulin production.

These observations are not supported by clinical observations or studies. One research team studied the relationship between sugar intake and conduct disorders, learning disorders, and ADHD in children. Behavioral and classroom measures were made after intake of sucrose, fructose, and placebo. The results did not distinguish the normal effects of increased energy intake from sugar effects, per se. Hence these investigators could not conclude that deviant behavior was increased by sugar.

Another sugar-challenge study in children reached the same conclusions. The investigator knew that some parents reported an increase in activity level when their children ate a high-sugar snack or meals and placed an advertisement in a local newspaper seeking children diagnosed as having ADHD with such an observed adverse reaction to sugar. Children were accepted into the study if they had ADHD and if the parents claimed an immediate effect of sugar on their children's behavior following smaller amounts of sugar than were to be given in the challenge study. There was no significant effect of glucose, fructose, or placebo on any of the behavioral measures either when the individual sugars were compared with placebo or when both sugars were combined. None of the behavioral challenges reported by the parents was observed.

Another researcher questioned if the effects the parents reported might be based on the blood glucose level and not on the intake of sugar. He designed a study in which children were given one of three breakfasts. One was high in carbohydrates, especially refined sugars; one was high in protein; and, one was high in fat. Following these meals, each was challenged with fructose, glucose, or placebo. He found that those children reported by their parents as reacting to sugar intake with an increase in hyperactivity did show an increase in activity level if they were challenged with glucose after eating a high carbohydrate meal.

It may be possible that refined sugars do increase the activity level of some hyperactive children if the blood sugar level is high enough. When the blood level of carbohydrates was high because of a high carbohydrate breakfast and the child was then challenged with refined sugars, the activity level increased. Possibly, it is the amount of a highly refined sugar product eaten over a brief period of time that results in increased activity.

Artificial Sweeteners

A recent study on aspartame (Equal or NutraSweet) suggests that some children with ADHD become more aggressive and noncompliant when given large doses of this artificial sweetener.

ADHD and Allergies

For many years pediatricians and pediatric allergists have reported that a higher percentage of the children they see with allergies have learning disabilities and/or ADHD compared with those children without allergies. Most studies have been done on the possible relationships between allergies and learning disabilities. Feingold focused on the possible relationship between allergies and ADHD. No studies to date have shown how allergies and this disorder relate. No treatment approaches have been confirmed to be successful.

Two clinicians have written about specific issues relating allergies to learning disabilities and/or ADHD and on specific treatment programs. Neither has presented research data that have been replicated by others; thus the proposed clinical findings and treatment approaches are not accepted by the general medical community. Because parents of children and adolescents with ADHD might read books written by these clinicians, their concepts and treatment approaches will be reviewed briefly.

Dr. Doris Rapp. Dr. Rapp believes that there is a relationship between food or other sensitivities and hyperactivity. She proposes a diet that eliminates the identified foods or the avoidance of other suspected allergens as a treatment for hyperactivity. She believes that the traditional allergy-skin testing for foods does not always detect the foods that cause problems. Her critics say that her sublingual-challenge tests are not valid measures of allergies.

Dr. Rapp identifies certain foods or food groups that children might be allergic to: milk, chocolate, eggs, wheat, corn, peanuts, pork, and sugar. She suggests that the parents try a specific elimination diet described in her books. This diet consists of eliminating all of the possible allergy-producing foods then adding one back each week to see if there is a change in behaviors. In her practice, she uses a food extract solution placed under the tongue to test for reactions. If the child is found to be sensitive to certain foods or to certain chemicals in the environment (e.g., paste, glue, paint, mold, or chemicals found in new carpets), these items are eliminated or avoided. She reports an improvement in the child's behaviors after allergy-producing foods and chemicals have been eliminated from the diet and chemicals from the immediate environment. Most specifically, she reports less aggressive or oppositional behavior and less hyperactivity.

Dr. Rapp's literature and videotapes of her testing children are impressive. On tape, a child sits in his parent's lap, happily interacting. A food extract solution of something the child has been found to be allergic to is placed under the tongue and within a minute the child becomes belligerent and very active. Still, other clinicians and researchers challenge her clinical reports and findings, noting that they do not get the same responses to the challenges nor the same benefits from the treatment. Thus her work is considered controversial.

I have seen patients who were evaluated by her and placed on specific elimination diets or monitored to eliminate exposure to certain chemicals who improved; that is, their level of hyperactivity and aggressive behaviors were lessened. On several occasions, exposure to the food or chemical resulted in several hours of hyperactivity and aggressive behavior. For some of these children, my clinical observations showed that the stimulant medication helped the ADHD; however, when exposed to the suspected food or chemical the hyperactivity increased. At this time, there is no final conclusion regarding Dr. Rapp's work.

Dr. William Crook. Dr. Crook has written extensively on the relationship between allergies and general health, learning disabilities, and ADHD. He writes about the "allergic-tension-fatigue syndrome." He also reports that specific allergies can result in hyperactivity and distractibility. Many of his more recent publications and presentations focus on the possible allergic reaction to a specific yeast and to the development of specific behaviors following a yeast infection. He reports that treatment of the yeast infection improves or corrects the problem.

No clinical or research studies have confirmed Dr. Crook's theories or replicated his reported clinical success. Here, too, the final answers are not known.

Summary

There is a relationship between brain function and nutrition as well as between brain function and allergic reactions. Clinically, these relationships appear to be as true for ADHD as for other brain disorders. Although research activity in these areas has increased, no consistent findings have been established.

There will continue to be proposed treatments based on these relationships. It is hoped that future research and clinical findings will clarify these relationships and will lead to better treatments for ADHD.

ADULTS WITH ATTENTION-DEFICIT HYPERACTIVITY DISORDER

Chapter 13

Adults With Attention-Deficit Hyperactivity Disorder

The exact percentage of children with attention-deficit hyperactivity disorder (ADHD) who continue to have this disorder as adults is not known. As noted throughout this book, studies suggest that about 50% of children will continue to have ADHD as adolescents and, of these adolescents, 50% (i.e., about 25% of children with ADHD) will continue to have ADHD as adults. Some follow-up studies show that 30–70% of children diagnosed as having ADHD continue to have either the full clinical symptoms or some residual symptoms as young adults.

Despite the clinical literature describing ADHD in adults and the follow-up studies into adulthood that show that it does not necessarily resolve after adolescence, the acceptance of ADHD in adults by the medical community is not complete. DSM-III included a diagnostic category called attention deficit disorder, residual type. This disorder described individuals who once met the criteria for attention deficit disorder with hyperactivity. No mention was made of the possible continuation into adulthood of hyperactivity or impulsivity.

In DSM-III-R there is no statement that an ADHD diagnosis cannot be used into adulthood, but there is no specific category for ADHD, residual type. However, there is the category, undifferentiated attention-deficit disorder. This is described as "a residual category for disturbances in which the predominant feature is the persistence of developmentally inappropriate and marked inattention that is not a symptom of another disorder, such as Mental Retardation or Attention Deficit-hyperactivity Disorder, or of a disorganized and chaotic environment" (American Psychiatric Association: Diagnostic and Statistical Manual of Mental Disorders, 3rd Edition, Revised. Washington, DC, American Psychiatric Association, 1987, p 95). This section of DSM-III-R makes reference to doubt that such a disorder exists and the comment, "Research is necessary to determine if this is a valid diagnostic category and, if so, how it should be defined" (American Psychiatric Association: Diagnostic and Statistical Manual of Mental

Disorders, 3rd Edition, Revised. Washington, DC, American Psychiatric Association, 1987, p 95).

At this time neither the stimulants nor the tricyclic antidepressants have been approved by the FDA for treatment of ADHD in adults. Thus, if they are used, the adult must understand that there are clinical studies supporting the use of these medications with adults who have ADHD and that these medications are approved for use with adults with other disorders.

Recognition

Few physicians who work with adults on health-related issues are aware of ADHD. Similarly, few psychiatrists or other mental health professionals who work with adults think of this disorder as a possibility when making a diagnosis. Thus it is often missed. These adults may be recognized when the clinician establishes the diagnosis in a child or adolescent and a parent says, "That's me. I have the same problems," or one parent points to the other and says, "He (she) is just like our child." Some adults recognize the possible reason for their difficulties when they read a newspaper or magazine article about an individual who discovered as an adult that he or she had and still has this disability. Fortunately, more college mental health services have become aware of ADHD in adults and recognize the behaviors when they see a student who has it. The following case example involves an adult who was first diagnosed as having ADHD in college.

Case 1

Fran was diagnosed as having learning disabilities in third grade. She had been in special classes through high school. During high school she had increasing difficulty doing her schoolwork. Teachers and parents complained that she would not stay on task or complete her work. She was in psychotherapy during her senior year and was placed on an antidepressant. She reported little benefit.

Fran went to a college that offered resource help and accommodations for her learning disabilities. However, she found the work difficult. She could not concentrate when she studied in the dormitory and became worried that she might not graduate. Fran went to the college mental health service at the advice of her former psychotherapist. The psychologist who saw her at the college suspected ADHD and referred her to me.

Fran gave a classic history of hyperactivity and distractibility throughout her life. She was fidgety and had been so "forever." Her friends, even her new ones in college, teased her about her constant need to move some part of her body. She described being distracted by any sound. She could recall examples from elementary school of listening to what was going on in the hall rather than in class. Fran cried as she described her impulsivity. She constantly hurt friends' feelings by saying something before she could think. Teachers always yelled at her for answering out of turn.

With Fran's permission, her mother was invited to a session. We asked her to bring all of Fran's old report cards and psychoeducational evaluations. The hyperactivity, distractibility, and impulsivity were described year after year, starting in kindergarten. The school and the parents assumed that these problems were part of her learning disability.

Fran was started on methylphenidate. At a dose of 10 mg tid she showed significant improvement. "It's a miracle. I feel so related. I can concentrate so much better, even in the dorm. I am getting my work done so much quicker and better. My friends have commented that I seem different. I pay attention when they are talking to me and I don't interrupt them when they are talking. Why was I not given this medicine when I was a child?"

As with children or adolescents who have ADHD, it is important to consider the related problems when establishing this diagnosis in an adult. Is there evidence of a learning disability? This disability may have been recognized when the individual was in school, as with Fran, or may have been missed. Furthermore, if the adult has emotional, social, or family problems, consider whether these difficulties might be secondary to or greatly impacted on by the ADHD and possible learning disability.

Diagnosis

As with children and adolescents, the diagnosis is made by establishing the presence of hyperactivity, distractibility, and/or impulsivity and by confirming that there is a chronic and pervasive history of these behaviors. The pervasiveness can be assessed by information provided by the individual. The chronic history might be confirmed by reviewing childhood and adolescent history, especially school history. Previous report cards and other school reports can be reviewed for evidence. If the parents are available, they can be asked. It is not uncommon to learn that this adult used to take medication as a child for "hyperactivity or for other related reasons."

Hyperactivity, distractibility, and/or impulsivity may manifest itself differently in adults than with children or adolescents.

Hyperactivity. This behavior may have been present when the individual was younger. It often lessens or stops by adulthood. If it remains, it is more likely to be in the form of fidgetiness. The individual, family, friends, and people at work will describe the constant level of activity. Some adults report that they are always active. They have difficulty relaxing or sitting still at any time (e.g., in the movies or at a restaurant). They also may have difficulty falling asleep at night and some report needing much less sleep than the average adult needs. Some find that the only way to relax and sleep is to exercise to the point of exhaustion. I have been surprised by the number of such adults who work out at a gym or run to the point of exhaustion each evening before coming home so that they can relax that night.

Distractibility. Distractibility is often the primary difficulty. This difficulty handling unimportant visual or auditory stimuli in the environment is the same as with children or adolescents, resulting in a short-attention span. Some adults report what appears to be more of an internal distractibility. They may have trouble organizing their thoughts or may report difficulty doing tasks that require them to keep track of many units of information at a time. Sometimes, this problem becomes a major issue with success on a job or a promotion. Suddenly, with the new position, the individual has more need to be organized or to manage details of information relating to himself or herself and to others. The distractibility interferes with success.

Impulsivity. Adults with this problem, like children or adolescents, may speak or act before thinking. They might say things before they consider the impact of what they are saying on others. They might act impulsively, thus seeming to have poor judgment. Some may appear to be more structured or compulsive than the average adult in an attempt to control their impulsivity.

Treatment

The treatment of ADHD in adults is the same as it is for children or adolescents. A multimodal approach including education, counseling, and the appropriate use of medication is needed.

Medication

As noted earlier, the use of the stimulants and tricyclic antidepressants has not been approved as a treatment of ADHD in adults by the FDA. Thus, the clinician must advise the individual before recommending treatment. The comments in this chapter on the use of medications are based on the my experiences. The approach to management of side effects, the initial medical evaluation, and the medical follow-up evaluations are considered to be the same as those for children and adolescents. Each clinician must consider each patient individually when developing a treatment plan.

The effectiveness of the group I medications (stimulants) does not appear to be related to body weight. I have had 200-lb men on 5 mg of Ritalin tid and young, 40-lb children on 20 mg tid. The issues of dose, frequency of dose, and time coverage with stimulant medication must be addressed in the same way as was discussed for children and adolescents in the previous chapters. The case example below illustrates the successful use of medication with an adult.

Case 2

Mr. S, a 30-year-old attorney came to see me after reading a newspaper article. He told me that he had been on a medicine from age 9 to 16 because of overactivity and trouble concentrating. He remembered that two of his sisters took the same medicine: dextroamphetamine.

During college and law school Mr. S was occasionally able to get this medication from friends. When he took it, he studied better and more efficiently. Currently, he was working for a law firm and having great difficulty staying on task and completing his work. He reported being frustrated with his performance. He knew he could do the work but had great difficulty staying organized and keeping track of "billable hours."

I restarted Mr. S on dextroamphetamine. At a dose of 5 mg every 4 hours he reported a dramatic improvement. He was able to concentrate and stay on task. His thoughts were more organized, and he became effective and efficient at work. His supervisors noted the change, as well.

If the adult responds positively to the medication, it is managed the same as it is for children and adolescents. Many adults report that they function better with their family in the evening and on weekends if they are on the medication and, thus, request taking the medication 7 days a week.

I have had a few adults with hyperactivity comment that they had become so used to living with this level of activity that they did not like the experience of being on medication. They say they felt too calm or sedated, or they report that they were so much more productive being hyperactive, working long hours and needing little sleep. They understand what the medication can do, yet they choose to stay off of the medication. I support this decision.

Counseling or Therapy

If the diagnosis is made as an adult and medication results in improvement, counseling, individual, or group therapy might be recommended to help these individuals understand themselves and the impact that ADHD has had on their lives. It is not uncommon to find established emotional problems that need to be treated. Similarly, the

ADHD behaviors may have had a significant impact on their social interactions, resulting in poor social and interpersonal skills. These issues also must be addressed.

If learning disabilities are present, the impact of this disorder must be addressed, as well. Perhaps these disabilities were recognized and treated when these individuals were children but no one has addressed the reality that these learning disabilities continue to impact on work and life demands. If these adults were not diagnosed as children, it will be necessary to explore how these disabilities have impacted on their education and career. Major interventions may be needed to help identify the areas of disability, the impact these disabilities have had and continue to have on them, and what can be done at this time to help.

Summary

It has been estimated that at least 25% of children with ADHD may continue to have this disability into their adulthood. It is important to consider this clinical possibility. The diagnosis and treatment is the same as it would be with children and adolescents. The secondary emotional, social, and family problems may be significant and need to be addressed. If learning disabilities are found, they too must be clarified and helped.

CONCLUSIONS

Chapter 14

Conclusions

Attention-deficit hyperactivity disorder (ADHD) is a life disability. It impacts on all aspects of life. For many individuals, ADHD is also a lifetime disability. Depending on the study used, between 25 and 70% of children with this disorder will continue to have symptoms of ADHD as an adult. Like any other developmental disorder, especially a developmental disorder that may be a chronic disorder, the consequence of not recognizing, diagnosing, and fully treating ADHD can be extensive. Each stage of psychosocial development can be affected as can academic success, self-esteem, and peer interactions. Significant emotional, social, and family problems can become as great a disability for the adult as the primary disability of ADHD. The secondary academic underachievement might impact on the work career and on work success.

Thus the recognition, diagnosis, and treatment of ADHD in children, adolescents, and adults are essential. Missing the diagnosis or not treating the disorder properly can result in a lifetime of disability. It is critical that health and mental health professionals know of this disorder and be alert to its possible presence. Of equal importance is the need to look for the associated disorders, especially learning disabilities. If ADHD has resulted in secondary emotional, social, and family problems, they too must be addressed. It is important to remember that the treatment of these difficulties will not be successful unless the primary disorder, ADHD, is identified and treated.

The treatment of choice is multimodal. Parent and individual education and counseling usually takes place first. Specific behavior management approaches might be needed. The use of appropriate medications is essential. Further individual, behavioral, group, and/or family therapy might also be necessary.

It is hoped that this book will be a useful clinical guide for the recognition, diagnosis, and treatment of ADHD in children, adolescents, and adults. It is further hoped that this book will help health and mental health clinicians work more successfully with children, adolescents, and adults with ADHD, as well as with their families.

Appendix A:
Suggested Readings

In keeping with the concept of this book as a clinical guide rather than a comprehensive textbook on attention-deficit hyperactivity disorder (ADHD), this section will not include an extensive list of journal articles and other literature. The reader can find such a bibliography in some of the references listed below. Because books are almost out-of-date by the time they are published, it is best for a reader who wants an extensive literature review on a specific topic covered in this book to do a computer search and obtain a printout of the most current information.

The suggested readings listed here are books that cover specific topics. Each book has a bibliography. The books listed first are those I believe to be most helpful; they are followed by books specific to each chapter.

General Suggested Readings

Ingersoll B: Your Hyperactive Child: A Parents' Guide to Coping With Attention Deficit Disorder. New York, Doubleday, 1988

> *Your Hyperactive Child: A Parents' Guide to Coping with Attention Deficit Disorder* is written for parents. The focus is on recognition, diagnosis, and treatment. Specific approaches and suggestions are discussed for parents to help their child.

Wender PH: The Hyperactive Child, Adolescent, and Adult: Attention Deficit Disorder Through the Lifespan. New York, Oxford Press, 1987

> *The Hyperactive Child, Adolescent, and Adult: Attention Deficit Disorder Through the Lifespan* is a book for parents and professionals. It reviews the diagnosis and models of ADHD treatment for children, adolescents, and adults. The section on adults is especially useful.

Weiss G, Hechtman LT: Hyperactive Children Grown Up. New York, Guilford Press, 1986

> *Hyperactive Children Grown Up* is a review of research started in

1961. The authors discuss their research as well as the research of others, focusing on known and controversial information. By using their long-term follow-up data, they try to identify patterns and use these patterns to suggest predictors that might suggest outcome. Of interest is a chapter on adults' views of their life experiences and their treatment as children and adolescents. A comprehensive bibliography follows each chapter.

Kavanagh JF, Truss TJ Jr (eds): Learning Disabilities: Proceedings of the National Conference. Parkton, MD, York Press, 1988

In 1986–87 an Interagency Committee was established by Congress to review and assess federal activities relating to learning disabilities. As part of this initiative, several experts in specific topic areas were asked to review the literature on their topic. *Learning Disabilities: Proceedings of the National Conference* includes each of these literature reviews. Several papers provide an extensive review of the literature on learning disabilities and language disabilities. The paper on hyperactivity-attention deficits is an outstanding review of the research literature on this topic. An extensive bibliography follows each section.

Silver L: The Misunderstood Child: A Guide for Parents of Learning Disabled Children. New York, McGraw-Hill, 1984

Published in English, Spanish, and Portuguese, *The Misunderstood Child: A Guide for Parents of Learning Disabled Children* is written for parents. It reviews the disorders of learning disabilities and ADHD. The history of each disorder is reviewed as well as how the problems are recognized and diagnosed. The major focus is on parent education, teaching parents to understand their child and to build on strengths rather than magnify weaknesses in helping him or her grow psychologically and socially. Parents are taught how to be advocates, fighting to get appropriate and necessary evaluations and treatments. Also, this book shows them how to become informed consumers, informing them about what is known about each disorder.

Barkley RA: Attention Deficit Hyperactivity Disorder: A Handbook for Diagnosis and Treatment. New York, The Guilford Press, 1990

In *Attention Deficit Hyperactivity Disorder: A Handbook for Diagnosis and Treatment*, Dr. Barkley has written an excellent and extensive review of the current literature on this disorder. In addition, he discusses in detail his research and concepts of ADHD. Chapters cover all topic areas covered in this book with a detailed discussion of research. There is a full bibliography at the end of each chapter.

Goldstein S, Goldstein M: Managing Attention Disorders in Children: A Guide for Practitioners. New York, John Wiley, 1990

Managing Attention Disorders in Children: A Guide for Practitioners focuses on assessment and treatment. The chapters on management, social skill training, and working with teachers are especially useful.

Silver L: ADHD: Attention Deficit-Hyperactivity Disorder and Learning Disabilities: Booklet for Parents. Summit, NJ, CIBA-Geigy Pharmaceuticals, 1990
Silver L: ADHD: Attention Deficit-Hyperactivity Disorder and Learning Disabilities: Booklet for the Classroom Teacher. Summit, NJ, CIBA-Geigy Pharmaceuticals, 1990
Silver L: ADHD: Attention Deficit-Hyperactivity Disorder and Learning Disabilities: Booklet for Physicians. Summit, NJ, CIBA-Geigy Pharmaceuticals, 1990

Each of these booklets offers a brief review of ADHD and learning disabilities for the reader noted in the title. Each relates to the other. For example, the Booklet for Physicians notes the need to obtain information from the teacher. The Booklet for the Classroom Teacher comments that the child's physician may ask for certain information, then explains what information to provide. Each is available to clinicians at no charge (and in quantity) from CIBA-Geigy Pharmaceuticals, 555 Morris Avenue, Summit, New Jersey 08901.

Specific Suggested Readings

Chapter 1: Introduction

Clements SD: Minimal Brain Dysfunction in Children. Terminology and Identification. Public Health Service Publication No. 1415, Washington, DC, U.S. Department of Health, Education, and Welfare, 1966
American Psychiatric Association. Diagnostic and Statistical Manual of Mental Disorders, 2nd Edition. Washington, DC, American Psychiatric Association, 1968
American Psychiatric Association. Diagnostic and Statistical Manual of Mental Disorders, 3rd Edition. Washington, DC, American Psychiatric Association, 1980

American Psychiatric Association. Diagnostic and Statistical Manual of Mental Disorders, 3rd Edition, Revised. Washington, DC, American Psychiatric Association, 1987

Shaywitz S, Shaywitz B: Hyperactivity/attention deficits, in Learning Disabilities: Proceedings of the National Conference. Edited by Kavanagh JF, Truss TJ Jr. Parkton, MD, York Press, 1988

Wender PH: The Hyperactive Child, Adolescent, and Adult: Attention Deficit Disorder Through the Lifespan. New York, Oxford Press, 1987

Weiss G, Hechtman LT: Hyperactive Children Grown Up. New York, Guilford Press, 1986

Chapter 2: Presenting Clinical Problems Suggesting Attention-Deficit Hyperactivity Disorder

Silver L: The Misunderstood Child: A Guide for Parents of Learning Disabled Children. New York, McGraw-Hill, 1984

Chapter 3: Establishing the Diagnosis

American Psychiatric Association: Diagnostic and Statistical Manual of Mental Disorders, 3rd Edition, Revised. Washington, DC, American Psychiatric Association, 1987

Shaywitz S, Shaywitz B: Hyperactivity/attention deficits, in Learning Disabilities: Proceedings of the National Conference. Edited by Kavanagh JF, Truss TJ Jr. Parkton, MD, York Press, 1988

Barkley RA: Attention Deficit Hyperactivity Disorder: A Handbook for Diagnosis and Treatment. New York, The Guilford Press, 1990

Chapter 4: Learning Disabilities

Silver L: The Misunderstood Child: A Guide for Parents of Learning Disabled Children. New York, McGraw-Hill, 1984

Johnson DJ: Specific developmental disabilities of reading, writing, and mathematics, in Learning Disabilities: Proceedings of the National Conference. Edited by Kavanagh JF, Truss TJ Jr. Parkton, MD, York Press, 1988

Tallal P: Developmental language disorders, in Learning Disabilities: Proceedings of the National Conference. Edited by Kavanagh JF, Truss TJ Jr. Parkton, MD, York Press, 1988

Ayres AJ: Sensory Integration and the Child. Los Angeles, CA, Western Psychological Services, 1989

Chapter 5: Associated Emotional, Social, and Family Problems

Barkley RA: Attention Deficit Hyperactivity Disorder: A Handbook for Diagnosis and Treatment. New York, The Guilford Press, 1990
Silver L: The Misunderstood Child: A Guide for Parents of Learning Disabled Children. New York, McGraw-Hill, 1984

Chapter 6: Etiology of Attention-Deficit Hyperactivity Disorder

Shaywitz S, Shaywitz B: Hyperactivity/attention deficits, in Learning Disabilities: Proceedings of the National Conference. Edited by Kavanagh JF, Truss TJ Jr. Parkton, MD, York Press, 1988
Barkley RA: Attention Deficit Hyperactivity Disorder: A Handbook for Diagnosis and Treatment. New York, The Guilford Press, 1990
Brown CC (ed): Childhood Learning Disabilities and Prenatal Risk. New Brunswick, NJ, Johnson and Johnson, 1983
Brackbill Y, McManus K, Woodward L: Medication in Maternity: Infant Exposure and Maternal Information: International Academy for Research in Learning Disabilities Monograph No. 2. Ann Arbor, MI, University of Michigan Press, 1985
Subcommittee on Reproductive and Neurodevelopmental Toxicology, Committee on Biological Markers of National Research Council: Biological Markers in Reproductive Toxicology. Washington, DC, National Academy of Science Press, 1989

Chapter 7: Basic Concepts in the Treatment of Attention-Deficit Hyperactivity Disorder

Goldstein S, Goldstein M: Managing Attention Disorders in Children: A Guide for Practitioners. New York, John Wiley, 1990
Barkley RA: Attention Deficit Hyperactivity Disorder: A Handbook for Diagnosis and Treatment. New York, The Guilford Press, 1990

Chapter 8: Individual and Family Education

Ingersoll B: Your Hyperactive Child: A Parents' Guide to Coping With Attention Deficit Disorder. New York, Doubleday, 1988
Silver L: The Misunderstood Child: A Guide for Parents of Learning Disabled Children. New York, McGraw-Hill, 1984
Silver L: ADHD: Attention Deficit-Hyperactivity Disorder and Learning Disabilities: Booklet for Parents. Summit, NJ, CIBA-Geigy Pharmaceuticals, 1990
Silver L: ADHD: Attention Deficit-Hyperactivity Disorder and Learning

Disabilities: Booklet for the Classroom Teacher. Summit, NJ, CIBA-Geigy Pharmaceuticals, 1990
Silver L: ADHD: Attention Deficit-Hyperactivity Disorder and Learning Disabilities: Booklet for Physicians. Summit, NJ, CIBA-Geigy Pharmaceuticals, 1990

Chapter 9: Individual, Parent, and Family Counseling

Ingersoll B: Your Hyperactive Child: A Parents' Guide to Coping With Attention Deficit Disorder. New York, Doubleday, 1988
Goldstein S, Goldstein M: Managing Attention Disorders in Children: A Guide for Practitioners. New York, John Wiley, 1990
Barkley RA: Attention Deficit Hyperactivity Disorder: A Handbook for Diagnosis and Treatment. New York, The Guilford Press, 1990

Chapter 10: Behavioral Approaches to Treatment

Gordon T: Parent Effectiveness Training. New York, Wyden, 1970
Silver L: The Misunderstood Child: A Guide for Parents of Learning Disabled Children. New York, McGraw-Hill, 1984

Chapter 11: Treatment with Medication

Shaywitz S, Shaywitz B: Hyperactivity/attention deficits, in Learning Disabilities: Proceedings of the National Conference. Edited by Kavanagh JF, Truss TJ Jr. Parkton, MD, York Press, 1988
Barkley RA: Attention Deficit Hyperactivity Disorder: A Handbook for Diagnosis and Treatment. New York, The Guilford Press, 1990

Chapter 12: Other Nonmedication Treatments

Feingold BF: Why Your Child is Hyperactive. New York, Random House, 1975
Conners CK: Food Additives and Hyperactive Children. New York, Plenum, 1980
Conners CK: Feeding the Brain: How Foods Affect Children. New York, Plenum, 1989
Rapp DJ: Allergies and the Hyperactive Child. New York, Simon & Schuster, 1979
Crook WG: The Yeast Connection: A Medical Breakthrough. Jackson, TN, Professional Books, 1986

Chapter 13: Adults With Attention-Deficit Hyperactivity Disorder

Weiss G, Hechtman LT: Hyperactive Children Grown Up. New York, Guilford Press, 1986

Wender PH: The Hyperactive Child, Adolescent, and Adult: Attention Deficit Disorder Through the Lifespan. New York, Oxford Press, 1987

Appendix B:
Resources for Professionals
and Families

There are many parent and professional organizations that are help-ful to clinicians, families of children and adolescents with attention-deficit hyperactivity disorder (ADHD), and adults with ADHD. Many of these organizations have state, county, and local groups. Local groups are most useful. Because such groups change in location or start new on a frequent basis, I will list the national office for each organization. The clinician or family can contact this national office for the location of the closest group or chapter.

PARENT ORGANIZATIONS

Attention Deficit Disorder Association (ADDA)
8091 South Ireland Way
Aurora, Colorado 80016
(800) 487-2282

This is a national alliance of ADHD support groups that provides re-ferrals and information to parents and parent support groups.

Children with Attention Deficit Disorders (CHADD)
1859 North Pine Island Road, Suite 185
Plantation, Florida 33322
(305) 857-3700

This is a national alliance of parent organizations that provides infor-mation and support to parents of children with ADHD.

Learning Disabilities Association of America (LDA)
4156 Library Road
Pittsburgh, Pennsylvania 15234
(412) 341-1515

This is a national organization with state, county, and local chapters for parents of children and adolescents with learning disabilities and adults with learning disabilities. It provides information on the disor-der and on available services.

National Information Center for Handicapped Children and Youth
P.O. Box 1492
Washington, DC 20013

National Information Center for Handicapped Children and Youth is an information clearinghouse that provides newsletters, fact sheets, issue briefs, brochures, booklets, and a listing of state and local organizations relating to different handicapping conditions.

PROFESSIONAL ORGANIZATIONS

American Academy of Child and Adolescent Psychiatry
3615 Wisconsin Avenue, N.W.
Washington, DC 20016
(202) 966-7300

American Academy of Pediatrics
P.O. Box 927
141 Northwest Point Boulevard
Elk Grove Village, Illinois 60009
(708) 981-7935

American Occupational Therapy Association
1383 Piccard Drive
Rockville, Maryland 20850
(301) 948-9626

American Psychiatric Association
1400 K Street, N.W.
Washington, DC 20005
(202) 682-6000

American Psychological Association
1200 17th Street, N.W.
Washington, DC 20005
(202) 955-7618

American Speech, Language, and Hearing Association
10801 Rockville Pike
Rockville, Maryland 20852
(301) 897-5700

Council for Exceptional Children
1920 Association Drive
Reston, Virginia 22091
(703) 620-3660

This organization includes an Education Resources Information Cen-

ter (ERIC) on handicapped and gifted children that provides informa-tion and a clearinghouse.

National Association of Social Workers
7981 Eastern Avenue
Silver Spring, Maryland 20901
(301) 565-0333

Orton Dyslexia Society
724 York Road
Baltimore, Maryland 21204
(301) 296-0232

OTHER ORGANIZATIONS

National Center for Learning Disabilities
99 Park Avenue
New York, New York 10016
(212) 687-7211

> *This organization provides publications and other public-awareness and public-education initiatives for parents, professionals, and the public.*

Self Help Clearing House
St. Claire's Riverside Medical Center
Pocono Road
Denville, New Jersey 07834
(201) 625-9565

> *This is a resource center that provides local and national referral ser-vices. A computerized data base of support groups and referral agen-cies nationwide is available.*

Index